BURNT TOAST:

Musings on living, loving
and saying goodbye

A collection of columns
Volume I

BY LENORE SKOMAL

Library of Congress Control Number: 2011907687
Lenore Skomal Press
Burnt Toast: Musings musings on living, loving and saying goodbye: A collection of columns by Lenore Skomal
Lenore Skomal. -- 1st Ed.
Volume I

ISBN-13: 978-1461156406
ISBN-10: 1461156408

Design by Judith Vorisek

Printed in the United States of America.

For Mom and Dad,
Gramps and Grandma Skomal,
Papa and Grandma Homoky and
all of my ancestors and friends whose lives
intertwined and impacted mine—
the result of which lies in these pages.

Also by Lenore Skomal

Lighthouse Keeper's Daughter

Keeper of Lime Rock: The Remarkable True Story of American's Most Famous Female Lighthouse Keeper

Heroes: Fifty Stories of the American Spirit

Secret Lives of Girlfriends

LifeLessons Series—Gratitude, Kindness, Forgiveness

The Power of Angels

Guide to Crystals

Wide Awake: The Insomniac's Guide to Ruling the World

Lady Liberty: The Untold Story of the Statue of Liberty

12,000 Dreams Interpreted

FOREWARD

It's a gift actually. I have been given the gift of space in the newspapers for which I write to entertain readers. Treating it as such has helped me dig deep and then even deeper to find something worthwhile to write about that can add another perspective, a bit of laughter or even some head scratching to someone's day. I treat each column I am allowed to write with dignity, integrity and sweat. That might sound odd or over-the-top dramatic, but it's true. I would have it no other way. I respect your time and appreciate your attention. It's the least I can do to make it worth your while to read me. Enjoy.

Lenore Skomal
Columnist

ACKNOWLEDGEMENTS

A heartfelt thanks to my husband Rick Sayers, who continues to be my primary muse and most avid fan, my son and my amazing family who have provided fodder all along the way and have yet to sue me, a loving hug to my friend and graphic guru, Judy Vorisek. I thank you and I love you all.

TABLE OF CONTENTS

CHAPTER I
THE CLEAN PLATE CLUB

BURNT TOAST

I'm told I am a baby boomer. Like others in this classification, I grew up at the hands of those who were shaped by the Great Depression and, thanks to that event, had developed quirky habits of obsessive thriftiness. Grandma was a fiend about saving bits of string and scrap paper. Mother washed and re-used tin foil until it got so crinkly, it fell apart. Then she kept the pieces in a kitchen drawer with about 50,000 unused twisty ties. I thought the behavior absurd, but knew not to question it, because I was just a kid. I had no rights. This was a time when the phrase, "Because I said so," was the height of positive parenting.

Waste was looked upon with disdain, so in my house, the one thing you never, ever threw away was food. It was sacrosanct. It was to be eaten, or recycled in the fridge for leftover night. Even burnt toast. Or should I say, especially burnt toast.

Back then, the average toaster was not as evolved as it is today. It had to be watched carefully, or, in the blink of an eye, a silky stream of black smoke would rise from its caverns, signaling yet another painful exchange with my mother. You see, I hated burnt toast. I hate burnt anything, but toast is especially stomach-turning to me. Surreptitiously, I would palm the blackened bread into the garbage. The ever-knowing eyes on the back of my mother's head would catch me.

"Do not throw that away! Burnt toast is good for you. It's good for your teeth. Just eat it."

I had heard this many times before. It was a very clever marketing strategy. Ever the well-behaved child, I would force the onerous thing into my mouth. Somewhere in the back of my mind, I felt secure in the knowledge that long after my body had been decimated by worms, my teeth would live on.

I think her ardent belief in the health effects of burnt toast stemmed from my grandfather. From the old country, he was an eccentric who worshipped regularly at toaster altar, burning bread willy-nilly and serving it up with relish—all in the interest of strong teeth. "The carbon is good for your teeth. It whitens them and makes 'em strong," he would pontificate. "Just eat it."

I clearly remember my grandfather's teeth: two perfect rows of uniform, white ivories. They sat in a glass on his night stand every night—crumbs of black carbon being scoured away by the industrious bubbles of Efferdent. They looked pretty darned strong to me.

Epilogue: I accidentally burned the toast the other day. My son made a face when I offered it to him. I felt his pain. But like any good mother, I told him: "It's good for you. Just eat it."

He turned to his father. "Just eat. It makes your hair curly."

CHOLESTEROL FIESTA

Remember when grease was a staple in every kitchen? You just don't see that anymore. I don't mean the kind of white, sanitized grease you buy in neat cylindrical cans. I mean the kind you make. It had to coagulate on its own into multi-layers of beige with fried food grit settled on the bottom. Frying bacon was our family's traditional method of making grease.

Stored in a slick-coated coffee can, it was pulled down from the top of the stove to make my mother's homemade donuts, to fry meats, to be added to a floury sauce for an added smoky flavor. So many uses. I think our grease addiction was hereditary, stemming from our Euro-ethnic and eastern block roots. My grandfather was a grease connoisseur, fond of whipping up his favorite Hungarian cookie recipe. As far as I could see, it was nothing more than two parts grease to one part flour; something akin to Moravian hard tack.

I remember a certain Saturday when my grandparents were visiting from the Bronx joined by my paternal grandmother—a died-in-the-wool Bavarian. It was raining, and someone got the bright idea to start cooking. It was a Cholesterol Fiesta. Mom fried off a hundred or so pounds of bacon just the get things rolling. The ethnic elderly went wild. At one end of the stove, my mother was busily frying up breaded veal, which would later be slathered with grease-enhanced sauce. She took the left over breading and egg and fried it up into large doughy balls for my grandfather, who was having a field day of his own with the oven, toasting up his brand of greasy cookies. "This is good grease, Irene," he added admiringly.

On the other end of the stove, my Bavarian grandmother—known the world over for her German potato salad—ladled warm lard and generous bits of bacon over a batch of steaming potatoes into an immense iron frying pan. My maternal grandmother, not much of a cook, siphoned off the now twice-used grease into several Chockful of Nuts coffee cans for latter use. Long after the cooking stopped, the grease hung in the air, forming a sort of marine layer in the upper atmosphere of the kitchen, where it clung to floating pieces of lint and eventually ended up clinging to the walls.

But like most addictions, denial accompanies abuse. After a lifetime of high cholesterol and high blood pressure, my grand-father died after suffering a series of debilitating strokes and heart problems. It couldn't possibly have anything to do with his alarmingly enormous ingestion of fats.

"He should have never smoked," said my mother, shaking her head as she scooped a large serving spoon of grease into the hot skillet. "Anyone for more potato pancakes?"

PIMP MY RECIPE

I wake up wondering about what I should make for dinner. Is that normal? Those who live with me–all male, even the dog–give me that 'tsk tsk' head shake when I broach the topic over their Wheaties. "What do you want for dinner tonight? Hmm? Chicken Marsala? Barbecue? How about Italian?" In response, I usually get the standard answer. "We can't even think about dinner!"

Well, I can. Clearly I am the only visionary in the lot. And I am not alone. My sisters do this, too. We think of meals all day long. We plan lunch before breakfast, dinner before lunch. It's hereditary—we get it from our mom. She was an unpaid, professional meal planner. She built her life around cooking dinner. With a regular houseful of 11 and many times more depending on which neighborhood waifs who wandered by, it's no wonder. Cooking the feast took hours. It took commitment. It took sweat-equity. It took smarts. She planned dinners for a week at a time, storing up groceries like gold bricks at Fort Knox. We had two food pantries, two refrigerators and an enormous chest freezer. She owned at least 50 cookbooks, and read them like novels, as if skipping one page would ruin the ending. James Beard would often accompany her on vacation. Bifocals perched, pen posed, she would systematically read page after page of recipes, making markings as she went.

Now years after her death, it is oddly comforting to flip through her cookbooks and find a legacy of advice and warnings. "Excellent!" one such note would read, with several exclamation points after it. "Double this" was written in script near the ingredients of another. If there was a slash through the recipe, avoid it like the plague.

It used to boggle my mind that regardless of how many times my mother made the same dish, she always referred to the recipe. You would have thought it would be etched in her mind. No winging it for her. Like a serious scientist conducting a sensitive lab experiment, she would measure and pour, stir not beat, preheat, saute and deglaze. If you interrupted her, she would drop her shoulders, look up at the heavens with exasperation, and say, "Now look what you've done! I've lost my place."

There were no cooking shows when my mother was alive–save Julia Childs, whom she hated because of her voice. If there were, she may have thought twice before she called the TV an "idiot box." Unlike my mother, I don't follow recipes. I am more of a hack; a chop-shop cook who strips a recipe down to its basics and then adds my own ingredients to suite my taste buds. My kitchen is a culinary version of the popular make-over show on cable TV that my son loves called "Pimp My Ride." I say, pimp my Chicken Cacciatore.

COOKING WITH GARLIC

My grandfather loved garlic. And because of that, my mother never cooked with it. She opted for powder and salt instead of using the raw bulbs.

Both things colored the way I was raised—never enjoying the full flavors of garlic until I myself began to cook and never liking my grandfather. Parents can do that to you. Their biases can be long-reaching. It was never that my mother openly railed against him or gave us a litany of the errors of his ways. When we were young, it was just a known fact—seen in their stiff embrace, stilted conversation and lack of smiles. It was a feeling more than anything else. But that oversensitive kid radar picked right up on it. Subtle was a paint that eluded my mother's brush.

The strange thing was, the older she got, it was as if the weight inside her life that clamped down on most of her true feelings about her parents and her upbringing, started to lift. Slowly, those emotions began to float upward, yearning for air. Once found, that air breathed life into them, and in the last years of my grandfather's life, the relationship became openly hostile. And in a guilt-by-association move, my mother began to take her anger out on her own mother as well.

When my grandfather died, my mother cooly directed me to take my grandmother to the funeral home to make arrangements. My mother refused to go. A college-aged me discussed the finer details of a casket, holy cards and burial costs as my grandmother wept quietly. She didn't speak on the ride home, but I did, fumbling once again to explain my mother's behavior with reasons I didn't have.

Her upbringing, while colorful, came out in spastic bits and pieces over the lifetime of knowing my mother—with long pauses of nothing where the affection for her father should have been. There were glimpses of cutting resentment in stories that were strangely vacant of detail, but full of powerful innuendo. There were allusions to unsavory behavior while drinking alcohol; two bitter estrangements from my grandmother which almost ended in divorce; bouts of unbridled temper outbursts; and just the vaguest of references to a bleak and disturbing side of this man who was my grandfather. Grandma bristled at my questions to unearth the truth. "It's in the past," she dismissed as she looked out the window.

I found a recent photo of Papa the other day, in my dad's things. His right arm twisted up and curled by his shoulder thanks to multiple strokes. But he was smiling—right into the camera which was inches away. I looked at him a long time, struck that I will never know this man or the reasons why his only child disliked him so much.

It's strange, every time I cook with garlic I still have to brush away a trace feeling of betrayal.

FREEZER BURN

"It's here, it's here!"

My mother jumped up and down with glee. Anticipation filled our little throats as the Sears deliverymen lumbered the immense rectangular box down the basement stairs. We hadn't been this excited since my father bought a new metallic green and gold swivel chair for the living room, and we played for hours with the box.

It was a chest freezer. It was the latest, most modern weapon in my mother's personal war against wasting food. Pride didn't goeth before the fall, uneaten lima beans did.

It quickly became the storehouse for leftovers. But it didn't take much time before my mother, who was driven to excess, to start freezing everything. Little and big bundles of meat wrapped in white waxed paper bound with freezer tape, every imaginable heat-and-eat bread, bun, and coffee roll; dozens of half gallons of sherbert, popsicles and ice cream sandwiches. She expanded the possibilities, treating the freezer chest like a cryogenics chamber. Cheese, bread, cold cuts, half gallons of milk, homemade cookies, sides of beef. If freezing were a religion, we were orthodox.

In no time, it was stuffed with food, all of it marked and dated with an indelible ink marker. I grew up sitting on provisions that could feed half of the state. It was a comforting thought.

My mother didn't ascribe to the inventory concept of FIFO —first in first out. Because the chest freezer was so deep, that you couldn't reach further than midway into its depths without falling in. On more than one occasion I would call for my mother, only to find her, legs akimbo, sticking out of the chest freezer. Whenever the provisions lowered to this level, she just re-stocked. Months after her death, we decided to tackle the chest freezer. I held my sister's ankles as she lowered herself to the bottom reaches of the chilly depths, and chiseled out the remaining white packages. "Pork chops, June 1976."

This turned me away from orthodoxy to reformist—I freeze only in moderation, never in excess. And as far as the refrigeration goes, I live by the 'eat it or toss it' commandment.

So it was with the greatest of shocks the other day I discovered way in the back of the refrigerator, a innocuous cardboard carton I had just assumed was milk. I turned it around and went numb.

Egg nog. I called my son.

"You need to open this." Face screwed into wince, he stuffed a dishtowel to his nose, and popped open the carton. Pork chops filled my head.

Relief and awe flooded his face. "Ma, it's fine."

I guess some things don't need to be frozen. Like diamonds, they're forever.

IN SEARCH OF JOHNNY MARZETTI

Have you ever eaten a straight egg? It wasn't until I was in high school that I realized that my family is most likely the only group of people on the planet who know what a straight egg is. It is not an egg that is attracted to eggs of the opposite sex. The origins of the straight egg died along with my mother, but I ate one almost every day of my childhood life. A scrambled egg without the scramble, a straight egg lies in the pan like a deflated omelet until flipped.

My mother also had a recipe for something called Johnny Marzetti—a mixture of pasta shells and meat sauce covered with cheddar cheese and baked in a large casserole dish. Again, I found myself bereft when trying to find this dish on a diner menu. A waitress once asked me whom it was named after. It had never occurred to me. Who was Johnny Marzetti?

There are so many other dishes that my mother lovingly created for us, which have padded the lexicon of our family history. Many times they didn't even have names. They were descriptive in nature: The Banana Dessert or The Hamburgers with the Cheese in the Middle.

It doesn't take long as you go through life to realize that your personal menu is something that only you and your family members directly share. In trying to explain to others, you oft times launch into a monologue describing exactly what The Banana Dessert is. You give up. Guess you just had to be there. So you trip merrily along life's past, eating other people's recipes, and waiting for the opportunity to meet up again with some morsel from your own past.

And then, one day at a fancy restaurant, you spy something called Bananas Foster. The description sounds happily familiar, and you wonder, could it be? Does The Banana Dessert really have a name? Now sitting in front of you is what looks like a gussied-up version of mom's fancy dessert. Primly sliced bananas in a puddle of caramel sauce topped with a swirl of cream. You go for the taste. Well, it certainly is tasty, delicious even. But....wait...no, no, it's definitely not The Banana Dessert. Mom smiles from above.

While I have yet to find any one who can replicate the tastes of my childhood, it's nice to try. I remember a long time ago, while visiting my mother-in-law, she offered me goulash. My Hungarian roots rejoiced at the mere mention of a steaming dish of gravied meat and potatoes. I thanked her for going the extra mile to cook up an ethnic meal for me. She look perplexed. "No, no, it's American goulash." American? I peered into the pot at the mixture of meat sauce and macaroni, and a sense of familiarity came over me. Could it be my old friend Johnny Marzetti? Doesn't a rose by any other name smell just as sweet?

BREAKFAST OF CHAMPIONS

I am the first one to admit that I am a little persnickety about keeping order in my kitchen. Mind you, I said persnickety, not obsessive. Since I am the one who uses the kitchen most of the time, I think I have the right to decide where everything goes. No one can argue with that.

This is not a hereditary trait. My mother could have cared less how you put things back in the fridge, or what shelf in the pantry you used. Food didn't have much of a shelf life in our house, what with nine people, three dogs, and half the neighborhood continually grazing there. It was stockpiled. We had two refrigerators, a chest freezer the size of a Ford Pinto and two pantries dedicated to foodstuffs. She must have figured, like French pigs on the hunt for truffles, we would find the food wherever it was.

While I can control where all the food is located, I can't seem to control the condition it is in. Sometimes I think I live with a band of starving people on the brink of extinction who, when my back is turned, frenetically hunt for food and rifle through cupboards with wild abandon. They can't get the containers opened fast enough. It's a common sight to see boxes toppled over and shelves in disarray in the wake of a feeding frenzy or the search for some particular item.

One continuing nightmare involves the seemingly innocuous task of opening a box of cereal. Cereal is something akin to snack food in my house. Take a look in any of my cupboards, and you will find boxes of cereal that look like a pack of ravenous mongrel dogs tore them open with their fangs. Is it too much work to actually unseal the cardboard tops gently so that the little tab can be inserted neatly into the slot? I believe that is the meaning of "reusable top." But those who live in my house just bypass the trying part. Pull out the box, firmly grip the edge of the boxtop, and rip that sucker open!

But wait! Not so fast. It's not enough to show that pesky boxtop just who's the boss. Now they have to deal with the sealed plastic liner inside. This must be most infuriating or perhaps it just challenges their manhood—for rather than simply slide out the plastic bag that keeps the cereal fresh, and pull open the lightly-glued seam, they'd rather tear a hole in the side of the bag like the Incredible Hulk on steroids. Anyone ever hear of scissors?

The result? A ravaged, topless box of cereal with a pile of spilled, stale cereal inside, sitting atop a dusting of sugary remains. Rather than complain, I simply take action. For if there is one thing I have learned from my family, it's going on the offensive is your best defense. I'm never buying cereal again. I wonder how a handful of uncooked oatmeal tastes?

MINT JULEP

It was my first mint julep and definitely my last. In Louisville, Kentucky doing as the Romans means trying to gag one of these bad boys down. During a recent trip to the famed horsetown of Louisville, we took a trip to Churchill Downs where the Kentucky Derby runs every May. Ever the adventuresome drinker, I lined up for my tall glass of julep, visions of plantations and Scarlett Ohara swirling in my head. I don't know what I was thinking. I must have assumed it would be minty and sweet. I forgot the main ingredient was Maker's Mark, a strong-tasting Kentucky aged bourbon. I hate bourbon.

But the burning feeling on my lips took me back to another time, a time when cocktails were so popular, they merited a party all to themselves. I was raised during that cocktail party era. And I am sad to admit I have many a fond childhood memory of them. Cocktail parties were as regular as Saturday night bingo.

Late in the day on Saturdays the excitement would build as my mother fussed about the kitchen in high heels, the living room awash with lemony Pledge. Ashtrays were pulled out of hiding, ready to be piled high with smoldering stubs. Highball and lowball glasses sparkled and placed neatly on the portable bar that rolled conveniently on castors. The sacred martini shaker was carefully examined by my father, the liquor sergeant.

Hors d'oeuvres were the make-or-breaker of a good cocktail party. Trays and trays of what would soon be hot edibles were stacked at the ready, shrimp and cold Aspeck salad chilled in the fridge, and fondue pots lined the buffet. Little crystal dishes of mixed nuts were placed strategically. And the bottles of booze were marched out, as my father lined up small compotes of cut limes, lemons, olives and maraschino cherries. Bourbon, scotch, whiskey and other brown liquor abounded. No one one ever drank wine and beer at a cocktail party. Chunks of ice were packed into fancy ice buckets waiting to be mixed into intriguing sounding cocktails like Whiskey Sours, Manhattans and Harvey Wallbangers. Or just used to chill the glass of the ever popular Martini. Mint Juleps weren't even on the radar.

Once the guests are arrived, the smell of hair spray competed with the lemony polish, and the laughter of women poured into their satin cocktail dresses mixed with the deep chuckles of the men and filled the air like a symphony tuning up. Ice tinkled in glasses and a thin layer of smoke rose to the ceiling.

I tasted bourbon back then as a teenager and spit it out. I tried it again in college, again at my parent's 40th anniversary party, again at a party right after my son was born and one more time last week in Louisville. My father always said that bourbon is an acquired taste. Well, so is liver. And I have managed to live without that all these years, too.

WAS IT SOMETHING I ATE?

Warning: This column could make you sick.

I just got over being "sick as a dog," as my mother would say. A strange saying since I think dogs in general are very healthy. In fact, my own dog is one of the healthiest living creatures I know, besides having some minor hip problems. But dog or no dog, I was sick. And it was the kind of sick that I truly hate. I was painfully sick.

There are some kinds of sickness that you can deal with, and still function. General malaise, feeling of unwellness, not a problem. A headache, common cold or irritating cough can be dealt with handily. Those things don't have to be anything more than a mere nuisance. I can handle those types of physical blips on the radar.

What I can't handle is any ailment having to do with nausea.

Thankfully, I am one of those in my family whom my mother also categorized as having a "strong stomach." Not six-pack abdominal muscles, mind you, but internally, tough as nails. No car, sea or airplane has ever gotten the better of me. Spicy foods and even graphic, gory materials don't upset this apple cart. So I guess when I get something like the stomach flu or eating contaminated chicken, I am just not used to feeling sick to my stomach. I truly hate that feeling. (In my wayward college days, the threat of a hangover was oft' times the best deterrent to keep me from tipping one too many.)

So when I was hit rather quickly with a bout of food poisoning recently, it was a slam dunk. On my back for days and whining to beat the band, I was the model patient. Searing abdominal cramps kept me from sleeping, but being a career insomniac, that didn't bother me so much. It was the nausea that was truly unbearable. I drank more ginger ale in one weekend than a small country. And since I abhor even the thought of relieving my stomach with what my dear friend calls the "technicolor yawn," I fought every sweaty inch of the way.

I am convinced that there are two types of people in this world: those who regurgitate and those who don't. Many, many in my family, including my son, fall into category number one. They have no problem with opening up their mouths and voiding. Not me. I am firmly entrenched in category number two. I hate it with such a vengeance, that I would rather white knuckle myself to an early grave than give in. Sometimes, like when I was pregnant with morning sickness, it was unavoidable. Or when I was a stupid twenty-somethingth and defrosted a package of chicken legs by placing them in the warmth of the kitchen window all afternoon. On those occasions, Mother Nature had other plans.

I have no idea why I am like this. Probably just pointless stubbornness, or as mother would say: "Just cutting off my nose to spite my face."

DAYS OF ICEBERG LETTUCE

Iceberg lettuce with spongy tomato wedges. Boxed frozen spinach and succotash. Canned corn niblets and Le Sueur peas. Celery and carrot spears, peeled and stuck in a plastic glass of water on the top shelf of the fridge next to my Grandma's prune juice. These were the vegetables I grew up on. And you wonder why I hated vegetables. My formative years were spent trying to hide lima beans in my napkin and mince spinach into nothing, in hopes of reversing the miracle of the loaves and fishes.

It wasn't my mother's fault. Fresh produce wasn't readily available when casseroles were king. And when it was, it certainly wasn't wasted on us. It was grown-up food, saved for the adults. What did a kid need with asparagus?

Time marched on and with it, experience. My mother taught herself her way around a stove, a student of Julia Child and James Beard. Eventually, she morphed into a fabulous gourmet, but that was after I had met my first salad bar at college.

Given my dearth of vegetable exposure and ingestion of casseroles during my youth, you would think I would have eating issues. While I obsess like most healthy neurotics, I do not have to deal with obesity. In fact, none of my processed, prepared-food-fed siblings struggle with their weight or health, either.

I mention this because in light of the expanding numbers of obesity-prone children, I pondered about what has changed since I was a kid. And that always brings up a lot of talk about the good old days, which if memory serves me, weren't that good.

Exercise is often cited as something that has been slowly replaced with sedentary hobbies, such as video games and the Internet. But is that all that different than the advent of television when I was a kid? I loved television, especially once my dad finally bought us a color one. While my mother derided it as being the "boob tube," it sure came in handy when she needed a babysitter. There was no limit on how much we could watch.

Sedentary was my middle name. If my mother had let us eat fast food, you could have put a "Mc" in front of that. But she didn't.

Never having eaten it as a child, I have to assume is why I have no taste for it today.

Food and exercise aside, maybe this issue is more complicated than that. As a child, I consumed pounds of tuna noodle bake, laid on my side glued to the idiot box for hours and ate nightly desserts and drank gallons of grape soda. I was no paragon of healthy living then.

Nor am I today, so I don't breathe rarefied air high atop my soap box when I say I worry about this ongoing debate. The issue shouldn't be about being fat but about being healthy, because if not we run the risk of creating a lot of collateral damage. Face it. Even thin kids can have low self esteem.

COOKIE CAKES

I miss wax paper. I discovered this longing recently when trying to recreate a freezer cake that my mother made in the late 60s and early 70s. It was a staple in the home of my youth, and one of two freezer cakes my mother gave as an option for our birthdays. One was affectionately known as the "ice cream cake"—not to be confused with the commercial, soft serve cakes that had yet to be invented; the other was the "chocolate cookie cake"—which consisted of two ingredients—whipped cream and chocolate wafers.

With a half-family reunion coming up, I decided to recreate both, since to my knowledge none of us has had one of these delicacies since my mother died almost 20 years ago. The ice cream cake was a snap, as the requisite four ingredients were easy to obtain. Well, I admit to substituting Bosco® Chocolate Syrup with Hershey's but my mother did, too. Much to my good fortune, Nabisco's 'Nilla Wafers were stocked at my grocery store.

But in searching for the ingredients for the chocolate cookie cake, I found Nabisco had left me hanging. I could not find FAMOUS Chocolate Wafers anywhere in the store. Much chagrined, I wandered to the baking aisle and had similar poor luck in finding Reynolds Cut-Rite Wax Paper. I left empty-handed.

My sinking fear was that both were discontinued. Had the simple chocolate wafers been replaced by swankier cookies because no one makes freezer cakes anymore? Did plastic wrap edge out wax paper, this once important staple of my mother's kitchen not to mention my playground? Who hasn't used a tear of waxed paper to grease a slide? I have fond memories of my school lunches of cream cheese and jelly sandwiches which were always tucked neatly inside a wax paper sandwich bag. After eating, the wax bag accompanied me out to recess so I could sit on it when I took my turn down the aluminum ramp.

What was strange was the discomforting feeling that overcame me. It was illogical really, but I truly felt that part of my childhood had been erased. It was as if some thief snuck into my past and ripped out pages of my happy memories. I was threatened with the truth: The cookie cake might be something my progeny will know about only through my foggy childhood tales.

As I is my habit in times of crisis, I turned to the Internet for comfort and direction. It didn't take long to realize I was not alone in my turmoil. I was surprised that so many had enjoyed the cake I believed was my mother's invention. I discovered it is formally called the "Famous Chocolate Refrigerator Roll" and those commenting on the sites were equally distressed in not being able to handily find chocolate wafers. Wax paper enthusiasts—those who hadn't migrated to parchment—were equally as upset. I contacted Nabisco and Reynold's and both emailed me a list of local stores.

I breathed a sigh of relief. My childhood is intact.

CAN OF SOUP

A can of tomato soup. It sits on my son's computer desk even as I write this—landing there after a circuitous trip that took most of the morning and included exotic stops outside the kitchen—the laundry room, linen closet, basement, home office and every hallway in between.

It was a slow morning of sorts that started with a cup of coffee in my hand. The same cup that somewhere along the way every day, gets placed on a counter, the dryer, or tank behind a bathroom toilet, never to be seen again.

When the phone rang, I was gathering up odds and ends scattered about various rooms intent on taking them back to their original and rightful homes. Now in the kitchen with the phone wedged under my chin, arms laden with homework, a stack of bills, old newspapers, a shirt needing to be ironed, and 12 pair of socks, I absentmindedly opened one of the cupboards, searching for something to eat for lunch. As I chatted away, I eyeballed the now infamous can of tomato soup.

Once in my hand, it was promptly forgotten. I must have slid it under my armpit as I placed the phone back in the cradle. There it stayed as I roamed from room to room, unloading my packages and organizing messes as I went. An hour or so later, after filling the cat dish and de-plating the dishwasher, I ended up in my son's room to deposit folded laundry. As is custom, I swept my hand over the dust on his desk. Annoyed, I dumped the rest of my parcels on the floor, except for the soup can which my body had now completely accepted as a new appendage. I dusted off the top, rearranged the pile of clutter into a neater pile of clutter, and in doing so, moved a bit too quickly. The soup can fell onto the carpet with a thud.

I stared blankly at it. Did it fall from another dimension? Was my father hoisting soup cans at me from heaven to get my attention? Did my son secretly hoard soup in his room, the start of a strange, yet disturbing pattern that could end up God-knows-where?

I stooped, picked it up and plunked it down on his desk, closing the door behind me to keep the cat out. Only then, on the other side of the door, did I stop and pause.

A can of tomato soup was under my arm pit while I piddled around the entire morning, and I ceased to notice it. Like looking for my glasses as they sit on the end of my nose or leaving the house in slippers, this soup can marked another misstep on the slippery slope of losing my mind.

I reached for the doorknob to retrieve it, but thought better of it. At least I'll know where it is when it's lunchtime.

CHAPTER II
MAMA KNOWS BEST

WHEN WE MEANS "YOU"

I call it the 'collective we.' And my mother used it with great ease when directing us to do chores or her bidding, yet she never once meant it. 'We' is the first person plural pronoun, indicating both you and me. When my mother started a sentence meant to be a command with the word 'we,' one might have erroneously assumed she meant both herself and the person she was addressing.

Not so. She meant only the person she was addressing. 'She' would never be part of the equation. "We need to clean your room today," meant a solo task was at hand that would not be remotely involving her. It was a polite way, I guess, of her telling us to do something by generously including herself in spirit but never intending that she be a part of 'we.'

I often taunted her back in the day about her liberal use of 'we.' I wondered aloud if when she used 'we' did she really mean just herself, as in the royal we? Perhaps she equated herself with the Queen of England known to use the royal 'we' when addressing her subjects, her reference to 'we' actually referring to both her and the Almighty.

"Mom, when you say 'We have to set the table,' do you mean you and God?" Her death stare suggested not. I would then smarmily ask her if her use of 'we' really meant she had multiple personalities, and in referencing 'we' she meant not only herself but her alter egos, too.

Oddly, she never thought that any of this was as uproariously funny as I did. To my mother, 'we' was simply an additional pronoun meaning the second person singular, or 'you.'

I was reminded of all of this over the Easter holiday, which I spent with my two sisters whom my ex-husband lovingly used to refer to as the Blister Sisters. Somehow, they have adopted my mother's grammatical dependency on 'we' when directing the tasks of the day. My older sister, clearly wanting me to mix up some onion dip for the masses, handed me a bowl and pointed to the fridge. "We need to make more dip." I waited for her to help but she left the room. Once again, I was part of a 'we' made up entirely of myself. We did as we were told.

At my other sister's house during Easter dinner prep, things were more fever pitch as the use of 'we' was thrown at me like balls in a game of Throwball. Orders for cooking food, serving platters, mixing drinks and watching children flew through the air, all preceded with the word 'we.' Again, the person hurling them around with such ease summarily abandoned all the tasks because the 'she' part of 'we' was busy doing something else.

So if you ever find yourself in a world where 'us' really means 'you' and 'I' is clearly absent, remember that 'we' always means 'me.'

AND YOUR MOTHER DRESSES YOU FUNNY

"You don't want to see yourself coming and going." It was one of my late mother's favorite fashion sayings. A veritable Coco Chanel, my mother was quite opinionated about clothes. She was a clothes-horse, with a collection of shoes that rivaled Imelda Marcos, complete with matching handbags.

If I were granted one wish, it would be to ask her this question: Where were you when I left the house? I look at photos of myself as a budding teenager, I wonder if she even glanced in my direction. I must have slipped through the cracks. Like most people, I pour over old photos of myself during those painful growing years of self-discovery, and can't help but wonder why my mother let me dress so poorly. It was just wrong. Especially with a father who was a shutterbug. Face it. There is nothing worse than coming of age in front of a camera lens. In the mid-70s.

In one particular photo, I'm wearing a timely red, white and blue T-shirt with a cartoon caricature of Spiro Agnew emblazoned on the front—political radical that I was at 12. I have on the most peculiar pair of brown corduroy, snake skin-print pants. My hair is stick-straight, parted in the middle and hanging down all around—very Joni Mitchell. If homeless were a look, I was the cover girl.

I remember that outfit—not just because it is forever chronicled in the family album but because it made me the laughing stock of the slumber party circuit. I walked in to my best friend's house for a sleep over. "You're screaming!" I turned crimson. "What do you mean?" It seemed to me that she was the one who was screaming. "Your clothes, they're screaming! They don't match at all!" I looked down dumbfounded. What doesn't match? Mother would be proud—no one clearly saw me coming.

It was enough that I became instantly oversensitive about clothes, and desperately afraid of being nabbed by the fashion police. In order to diminish my chances of making another fashion faux pax, I opted for the conservative-bordering-on-cloistered look: solids, dark colors, blindly picking my way through the complicated world of mix-and-match. I blessed my parents every day for sending me to parochial school where a uniform was required. How can you mess up socks and shoes? I briefly considered a life as a nun, but realized that fear of dressing myself would not constitute getting the calling.

My own fear was exacerbated by my mother's belligerent fashion sense. She was my antithesis: bright, shocking colors, with nary a care about being too flashy or overdressed. It wasn't until years after she died that it dawned on me: Mother didn't have any fashion sense at all. She just wore what she wanted, called it fashion, and the rest of the world be damned. That's why she never saw herself coming and going.

I'm working on that, but I'm still not there yet. Perhaps if I were, I'd give those corduroy snake skin pants another whirl.

DON'T NEEDLE ME

Like most humans I dislike pain immensely. But I do agree that the anticipation of it is worse than the actual thing. In fact, when it comes right down to it that's the part I hate. I have a zero tolerance policy for pain-anticipation. If it's going to hurt me, don't tell me about it beforehand, just do it. My mother understood this concept. When it came for our regular visits to the doctor, she kept mum, even fibbed about the ever-looming possibility that a shot might be involved. Our family doctor was affectionately known to us as Father John, although I think he was Protestant. There'd we be, piled up in the back of her 60-something Rambler station wagon, tense with the anticipation that at the end of the ten minute car ride, one or all of us could be facing pain. My childhood just seemed like an endless series of inoculations.

For some reason, I was often first in the barrel when we got to Father John's office, which I guess was good. Out he would come to the waiting room, and call my name, looking unsure about which one I was. Even though he was a good friend of my parents, he never seemed to be able to link our names to our faces. Like other adults, he could only identify the oldest one or two, but after that, we were just a conglomerate of look-a-likes, generically addressed by 'honey' or 'son' depending on gender. Tentatively I'd turn back to my mother, and whisper, "Am I getting a shot?" She would shake her head emphatically, and whisper back, "Just get in there."

Dutifully, I'd scoot up onto the checkup table and have my 'physical:' knee reflexes were checked with the small rubber hammer, lungs listened to with a stethoscope, chest rapped firmly with the tips of his fingers, and eyeballs examined with a penlight. Fairly high tech stuff. If lucky, that would be it. But luck often eluded me. Holding my breath, I'd watch as Father John went slowly over to my chart. He'd walk over to me, his arm concealed by his side. "You're due for a shot." Oh god. No sooner were the words out of his mouth, then the thin, steel syringe appeared in his hand, in my arm and out again.

Back in the waiting room, I'd eyeball my mother, rubbing my upper arm. She'd shrug. "Well, you have to admit, he does give a good shot." I wasn't a needle connoisseur at the time, but now with years of dealing with assorted needles, shots and blood donations behind me, I have to admit, Father John did give a good shot. Why? He had mastered the element of surprise.

HAND HUGS

I confess, it's the one thing I will never get used to. In this life's calling know as parenting I will never understand why our children, for a prolonged period in their lives, find us embarrassing. I'm a fairly critical person about my shortcomings, but I would rarely describe myself as embarrassing. It happened so suddenly. Almost overnight any show of affection displayed outside of home is not only taboo, it's the height of embarrassment. I can see how slapping a big, sloppy kiss smack-dab on the lips can be embarrassing. But should asking 'How was your day?' prompt a withering look? It leads the astute parent to assume the correct protocol in public is to completely ignore them. When picking them up from school or a friend's house, walk stick-straight, well in front of them, and silently slide in the car, like robotic servants programmed to guide their pre-pubescent masters home.

And then, when the doors to the car are shut, sufficiently sealing the cone of silence, are you allowed to show affection. A little tousling of the hair, a good-natured shoulder hug is acceptable a small kiss is tolerated; though not often returned.

During one of these rides home, my nine-year old was genuinely puzzled about his good friend's mother. "I think she really likes to embarrass him," he said, quite innocently. I started laughing. "It's not funny. She actually walks him into class everyday and stays there until he unpacks his books and everything." I shook my head as if empathizing, knowing in my son's ideal world—the Never-Never Land of the Lost Boys where nary a parent can be found—this is an egregious offense. I, on the other hand, am by now well trained. I just wave from a distance when dropping him off. "Well, maybe she loves him very much," I ventured. "If she did, she wouldn't embarrass him," he replied. In this parenting thing, you can't win.

As we drove along, a memory of the cute toddler-baby dislodged itself from my memory banks and floated to the surface. I heard the tiny voice of the one who used to cry so sadly in his car seat behind me, because he wanted to hug me, but couldn't because I was driving. I would stretch my arm way back and clasp his tiny hand in mine, and say, "See, we are hugging! We're hugging with our hands!"

As we left the car to cross the street to the grocery store, I took his hand, as is the rule. We crossed the intersection, and once safely across, did I imagine it? Or did this grown-up boy let his hand linger in mine for a few extra minutes, giving me a hand-hug?

ROOM MOTHER

There were many things I wanted to be when I grew up. Being a room mother was not one of them. In the world of volunteering at your kid's school, most mothers know the competition is stiff. The women who dominate the power clique known as the Parent's Association at my son's grammar school keep an iron grip on entry. It requires a regal bloodline, a Papal nod or the signing over of one's soul.

I've seen this before, possibly most acutely in high school within a tightly-knit group of blossoming lassies known as cheerleaders. Like cheerleading, you don't volunteer for the PTA. You are chosen.

It seems that my PTA has provided a catchall for that cluster of people whom, in their collective psyche, never left high school. A lot of them were captains of the football team, presidents of student council and of course cheerleaders. While I personally ran screaming from high school, they basked in their glory days.

Class reunions underscore this. Several years ago, I withered in empathetic embarrassment when a bunch of former cheerleaders—aging yet smiling—actually pulled out the poms-poms, so to speak. I was waiting for the pregnant one to scurry into position at the bottom of the pyramid.

It appeared to me that like-kind was running our parent's association. A puny nobody back in high school, I learned to leave cheerleaders alone. I left this crowd alone, too, especially after my efforts to volunteer were summarily ignored.

But one afternoon I was waiting to pick up my son outside, which is a particularly gay time for the inner circle who arrive a half-hour early, coffee cups in hand. I was entertaining myself with an irreverent fantasy of arriving at the crowd's fringe, toting an open bottle of Wild Turkey and interjecting a breathy Whazzup?, when it was daydream interruptus. I overheard the head cheerleader say she couldn't find anyone to be room mother for the fourth grade. Odd, I thought, since my class seems chockful of tow-headed women who would look great in saddle shoes.

"No one asked me," I thought out loud. You'd think after all these years you'd know your place. An itchy, high-schooly feeling overtook me and I had the strange urge to pull up my knee socks and go hide in my locker.

"I'll volunteer," I ventured. Oh that's funny. I kept talking. What the hell. The head cheerleader was stunned. "We'll get back to you." As I walked away with my son, I turned back to her. "It's okay. I understand. I really do. I was never a cheerleader, either."

Later that day, she left a message for me. "You can be a room mother if you want."

I was puzzled. Maybe she had never been a cheerleader either.

THE RABBIT DIED

Warning. This column is based on a true story. It contains graphic scenes, and is not meant for small children, the faint of heart, or women who liken pregnancy to tripping the light fantastic.

Someone I know is planning to have a baby. It is so exciting. The planning, the anticipation, the joy. The pregnancy.

I had heard about morning sickness. I had been nauseous before. To call morning sickness nausea, is akin to calling T-Rex, a lizard. I wasn't just sick to my stomach; my pores were nauseous. Innocuous things like air, color, sounds and thoughts, or activities like walking, breathing, standing still and sleeping, launched a roiling queasiness. It was like living in the "Perfect Storm" for five months. And I don't know who started the saltines myth. Dry crackers gave me dry heaves. Nothing worked. And all the time I wished so badly that I showed, so everyone would understand my suffering. I also longed to don my pregnancy outfits.

By the time the nausea ended, my wish had come true. My tummy was growing. And I kept on growing and growing and growing. I recall my mother's tight, little basketball tummy. And that was pregnancy number seven. I looked like I swallowed a hot air balloon, and in the process, the escaping gas inflated my face and appendages into freakish proportions. When I sat down, my navel was even with my nose. Since my caregivers graduated from the "Eat Your Weight in Protein and Then Some" school of pregnancy thought, no one blinked. They were happy. I felt proud.

It was around my seventh month, that the weight became so unwieldy, I couldn't maneuver it anymore. No position, except crawling around on all fours, was comfortable. Walking a short distance set off an asthma attack. I couldn't breathe. My protrusion entered a room several seconds before I did. And it moved.

Sitting at work, my stomach served up before me like a great feast, slow huge waves of movement would commence, like a sperm whale moving through the ocean. The bachelor boys at work would stare like jacked deer. "It's moving." The kid moved then like he sleeps now, athletically and constantly.

By the beginning of my eighth month, I was done. I knew if things were tough now, they weren't getting easier. It wasn't like I could lose weight, or take muscle relaxants, afterall. Get this over with. Bring on the labor, I thought.

After all, how painful can that be?

MY BODY BELONGS TO THE WORLD

I'd heard it said that when women get their breasts enlarged, they often have no problem with people touching them. I found that hard to believe until someone I know got hers 'done.' Pre-enlargement, she was as possessive of her body as most of us women who don't professionally strip for a living. It's not that we shrink from the touch of strangers, but there are certain 'okay' zones, which include anything on or about the shoulders and upper back, and all parts of the arms, except the pits. Anywhere below the neck on the frontside is off-limits, down to and including the feet. And the breasts!? Not an option for stranger touching.

Obviously my friend is very proud of her new look, as she is well at ease with offering friends a peak or a squeeze. I wonder what happened to make her so bold. Is it because they're stuffed with plastic so they don't feel 'real' to her? Or maybe it has to do with the fact they stick out so far from her body. It's like a pregnant woman's stomach—located so far in front of the rest of the flesh-and-bones structure, it doesn't even feel like it's still you. It somehow begs to be touched.

I remember that feeling well. I recall being in the grocery store, well into my third trimester. I was moving like Cyclops through the aisles, my stomach acting as a wrecking ball, swinging on its own in front of me. Salt cod and warm diet ginger ale were on my mind—a tantalizing taste combination worth obsessing about. My stomach rounded the bend, only to find several old women blocking the refrigerated fish case.

"Ooooh, how many months?" someone chirped, as the cluster of blue-haireds flitted around me. "I'm seven months along," my words pumping out on a breathy-slide, as I maneuvered my 50 lb. stomach toward the salty stacked fish. But in the blink of an eye, my protuberance was seized.

"Oh, the baby's kicking," they circled me now, like a frenzy of baby-starved women. I tried to wriggle away from the invasion of bony hands, but they kept rubbing my tummy and chattering. "It's a big baby." "I think it's a boy!" Thankfully, the novelty soon wore off and the assault ended as quickly as it began.

I plucked my pack o' salt cod from the case and pitched it in the cart. By the time I made it to the check out, no less than four other women had cornered me, boldly patting my bulbous stomach. In that moment, like Madonna and perhaps my busty pal, I resigned myself to the ultimate truth. My body now officially belonged to the world.

MY LIFE AS A TRASH CAN

It didn't take long for me to realize that my primary responsibility as a mother is to be a garbage receptacle. It comes on fairly early in the mothering process. Once you start leaving your house, in fact. Every trip requires an extra arm to lug the diapers, bottles, what have you. And once your tiny urchin has started packing away real food, the scene is now set, for food comes with packaging. You're marked from the first time you absently stuff the waste into your pocket, to get back to the joy of gazing at your child gumming Saltines.

The awe quickly fades, but the trash keeps on coming. The baby soon grows out of baggies filled with Cheerios and into juice boxes, tiny packages of raisins and snack bars. Then it's on to chips, plastic bottles of Powerade, ice cream bars and Subway sandwiches. All the while, your pockets keep growing.

To this day, when the seasons change, I pull out my old faded winter jacket and thrust my hands into the pockets to inevitably find a treasure trove of litter. There's always at least two blue screw-off plastic caps which housed some chemically-colored drink ingested by my progeny the year before; a flattened bag of Fritos still slick from the oil in which they were processed; a few errant corn curls wedged into the bottom of the pocket, surprisingly fresh; a broken and chewed Popsicle stick; and an empty pack of gum. Wait a minute. My child doesn't chew gum. Whose garbage is this?

Motherhood ensures you a lifetime of pockets stuffed with not only the refuse from your own child, but every child. Nieces and nephews, friends' children, children's friends, even your own husband—view you as the keeper of the trash.

My son is now 10, and fully capable of discarding his trash himself, as are his friends. But, like the Statue of Liberty, I must be telepathically calling for wretched refuse.

While at my son's baseball game this summer, a small child was peeling the plastic wrapper off a particularly uncooperative piece of candy, while his teenaged babysitter sat in utter boredom nearby, staring out to some distant land. I watched as the wee one wrestled the candy into his mouth. He looked panicked as he searched for some place to rid himself of the sticky wrapper. Perhaps it was my pockets, which looked oddly flat sans their usual wad of refuse. Or maybe it was that maternal look I wear—the one of passive acceptance of my lot in life.

He ran up to me and said what children everywhere must view to be the magic word in these situations. "Here." I accepted the offering, stuffed it in my pocket and sighed. Once a garbage can, always a garbage can.

GRANDMA LOST

"Oh I just love that age!" Have you ever heard someone say that when they see a newborn or a cute toddler? "They are just so cute at that age." Why doesn't anyone ever say that about teenagers? "That is such a great age!"

I guess I am lucky. I have always enjoyed all the stages of my son's growth. Even the tantrummy times when his little face would turn beet-red as he emitted howls something akin to a devil's cry from hell. Even then, as his head spun right off his shoulders, I never wanted him to be any other age than what he was. I loved watching him grow.

Now as I adjust the rearview mirror and watch him and his pals singing the words to some gangsta rap hit, I revel in how this kid got to where he is.

Early on I spent a lot of time convincing myself to accept the reality that some day my son would grow up and leave home. Toward that end, I adopted the healthy habit of accepting and not fighting his growing up. Sounds frighteningly mature, doesn't it? It is part of my mothering credo: smile and nod on the outside, scream like a derranged banshee on the inside. Never let 'em see you sweat. Works like a charm.

I think it works. My son had, as part of some homework assignment, to list his long-term goals. To his ten-year-old mind, writing out a Christmas list is a long-term goal. The category was family. "Mom, do I want to have my own family?" I told him I wished he would, already envisioning my grandbabies propped on my knee. "Is raising a kid hard work?" I laughed and looked at him, as if this were a rhetorical question. Was he serious? Yes he was. I told him in the affirmative. He looked down at his homework assignment. "Scratch that. I don't need any kids."

With all those grandbabies wiped off my knee with an erasable pen, I stood pondering. There really is something to this concept of making something look easy.

"How about being married? Is that hard work?" Again I looked at him. "Well, if you think raising a kid might be hard work, you might want to put marriage in that same category."

"I like being alone," he said complacently. I should've lied to this child. Visions of him living home until he's 50 raced through my mind, both of us running the Bates Motel. Or worse yet, he might end up like my brothers—bachelors for life.

COME DANCING

The average marriage lasts 10 years. That's a statistic I heard recently, but people must have suspected this for a long time. Years ago, I knew a couple who entered into their marriage like a leasing contract, maintaining their option to renew after 10 years. At the time, I was very single, very young and privately aghast at the arrangement. But in light of these news stats, maybe it made sense.

I did a little bit better than the odds. My son's romance with me lasted exactly 12 years. Okay, it's not exactly a marriage, I know. He was only five when he popped the question. But it was one of those mother-son moments that you will carry with you to the next life. I was putting him to bed one night, he turned his little face up to mine as I bent down to kiss him goodnight. "Mommy, will you marry me?"

I suspected this was coming. I said, "Of course I will. When you are 18 years old, honey, if you still want to marry me, ask me again." He can't even legally stay home alone yet, but it would appear the honeymoon is over.

Sometimes, you just don't see the end coming. It was last Friday night and we were all getting ready to head out to his school for a family sock hop. We envisioned a fun evening, one with all of us dancing and laughing. As he brushed his hair—a startling new development signaling teenagehood—he turned to me, and said hesitantly, "Mom, I don't think I have to say this, but please don't embarrass me tonight."

I could tell by the way his eyes evaded mine, he was not joking. Oh well, there goes the naked dancing across the tables. Better leave the lampshade home tonight. I remember being embarrassed by my parents at his age—but I had good reason. My parents weren't exactly wallflowers. Fuschia was a staple color in my mother's wardrobe, and my father thought an ascot was a fashion must.

After recovering from my general shock, I cornered him. Did I often embarrass him in public? The man-boy hedged and mumbled something about no, no, this was not about my general behavior. (Whew!) This was about making sure I didn't embarrass him by dancing at the event.

Never knowing when to leave well enough alone, I pressed. "You know, there was a time, mister, when you loved to dance with your mother. I was the one who taught you how to dance. " I was then informed that no parents would be allowed to dance, and certainly if they were, it wouldn't be with their children. Our role was to "watch."

After spending the night "watching" my son ask girls to dance with a confidence I never had at his age, we drove home and I thought of that little moonlit face peering sheepishly up in the night so long ago. I asked him if he remembered. He smiled his little boy smile. "Yeah. Thanks for saying, yes."

POLITICALLY CORRECT

I remember when I was pregnant with my son. Not knowing what gender he was, I decided after reading all kinds of books about the deep connection between baby and the mother-womb, that I would figure it out myself by listening to my inner sage. After many deep ponderings, I convinced myself he was a girl. So certain was I, I picked out his name, a beautiful little girl's name—"Camille," and even told my friends. They purchased pink, soft baby outfits, which I laid out on top of the changing table. I gave merely a passing thought to a boy's name.

When he was born, I am sorry to say, my first words were, "What do you mean a boy?!"

Determined to raise this child as politically correct as possible and unfettered by the sexual roles imposed upon society, I had already made decisions about what would be acceptable toys—if he had been a girl. NO BARBIES was one of them. As a neophyte mommy, I was utterly opposed to this doll which represented everything that I am not. My daughter would be exposed to non-discriminatory role models. She would learn about rebuilding car engines, and all of those things that I naturally avoid. But, of course, there would always be shopping, with the ever-vigilant eye for value.

So when my daughter turned out to be a boy, I was confused. Just shift gears, I thought. I bought him a doll house. It was stocked with new furniture—the expensive, collector's kind—and I searched for family-oriented little figures. There it stood. And it stood. Collecting dust. Untouched for a long while, until his uncle gave him a squirmy, fake snake for his birthday. All of a sudden, the house was the center of attention. The house was under siege. The snake slithered through windows, destroying furniture and slaying its inhabitants. Those who weren't rendered dead, were stuffed into the refrigerator, cabinets or oven. I stood, appalled. Nature or nurture?

Alas, opinions, like underwear styles, change with age and ma-turity. The dollhouse—sans snake—eventually found its way to my niece's bedroom, where a tiny mommy serves up tea every afternoon and the furniture is carefully dusted. It has since been replaced in my son's room by a siege tower and multiple knights, thousands of small green army men and an arsenal of weapons. And—I am chagrined to admit—that GI Jo, Barbie's male counterpart, regaled in fatigues and draped in hand-grenades, sits perched on the windowsill, ready to pick off any enemy who wanders by.

In a feeble attempt to cling to my own once-staunchly-held principles, I must say here: I personally have never shelled out one thin dime to buy a Barbie for any child. That has to count for something.

MURPHY'S LAW

Some people live their lives following the laws of the land. Others find direction and solace living by the Golden Rule. Still others abide by the laws of their church, believing that organized religion brings order to society. Me? I believe in the laws of nature. I follow Murphy's Law. Like gravity, there is no denying Murphy's Law, for if anything can go wrong, I have found that it will. And if things appear to be going smoothly, you obviously overlooked something.

In search of the origin of Murphy's Law, I found an article from *The Desert Wings*, March 3, 1978. It says that Murphy's Law was born at Edwards Air Force Base in 1949. It was named after Capt. Edward A. Murphy, an engineer working on Air Force Project MX981, a project designed to see how much sudden deceleration a person can stand in a crash. One day, after finding that a transducer was wired wrong, he cursed the technician responsible and said, "If there is any way to do it wrong, he'll find it." The contractor's project manager kept a list of "laws" and added this one, which he called Murphy's Law. Actually, what he did was take an old law that had been around for years in a more basic form and give it a name.

Murphy's Law appeals to my love of bite-sized quotations and what I generally call bumper sticker philosophy. You'd be amazed at how many truths live on the backsides of mini-vans and beat up Buicks. You can learn so much about the world, politics, ex-wives, vegetarianism, Smith & Wesson and fishing. One of my favorites is, "Drive like you stole it." But that's another story.

Another reason I like Murphy's Law is because it's true. I know this because I live it every day. Doesn't it always happen that the one day I am running really, really late for an appointment, guess who hits all the red lights? And of course, since the only things that start on time are those you are late for, I am late. Never fails.

In that vein, I have created my own corollaries to Murphy's Law.

- If a tree falls in the woods it will most likely be on me.

- Blizzards only hit on grocery shopping day.

- Bad things come in threes. Good things, however, travel solo and often miss my exit.

- It's when you need to knock on wood you realize we live in a plastic world.

- Ignorance is not only bliss, it's essential when raising teenagers.

- Be careful about keeping an open mind. You never know what could fly in.

- The degree of stupidity of your actions is directly proportionate with the number of people watching.

- When asked to do a chore, the first question out of every child's mouth will inevitably be either "What?" or "Why?"

Murphy's Law is sobering, asking one to prepare for the worst. But it also encourages one to appreciate the present, because as Murphy himself would say, "Smile, tomorrow will be worse."

ODE TO GEORGIE

The black and white photo, yellowing and fading, has been no stranger to me. It sits with a series of similar shots in an old fashioned photo album, neatly tucked into felt, triangle corners. The 3-year old boy in the photo is squinting in the sun, his arms outstretched against the pipe railing of the Boardwalk in Atlantic City, circa 1939. It's my mother's little brother.

My mother rarely spoke about him, even when asked. The few stories I was able to eke out of her had to do with spending days at the shore, pampering her toddler brother and taking him to go see "The Wizard of Oz" when it first hit the silver screen. She was 14 at the time. At my wedding, I danced to "Somewhere over the Rainbow" with my father. And my mother cried. It was to honor Georgie, my dead uncle.

Some of the spotty details about Georgie's short life included vague, ugly references about how my grandfather wasn't very nice to him. Of course, this wasn't surprising since he wasn't very nice to any of us grandchildren. But my mother's eyes smoldered black when she recalled those days.

It was my belief Georgie died after that summer at the shore—a victim of pneumonia, I thought. In the album, there are no more photos of him. All I remember is my mother telling me he died. Her only brother, her only sibling. And she would miss him until the day she died, which she did.

My grandmother, on the other hand, refused to discuss the "baby" at all. When we reached the pages of the dog-eared photo album with those summer photos, she would quickly turn them with tears in her eyes and ended whatever questions hung in the air with a simple truth: he was dead.

It wasn't until a conversation with my older sister that I discovered the truth. Georgie did not die that summer. He was given back to the system. Georgie was not my mother's biological brother nor my grandmother's son. He was a foster child.

"Didn't you ever wonder why Georgie suddenly appeared in the photo albums at the age of three?" she asked. No, I never wondered. In our family, there are barely any infant photos of my younger brothers and sisters. Number one got all the face time with the camera and interest waned with the birth of the rest of us.

My grandfather gave him away, over the emotional protests of his wife and daughter, which explained a lot. It explained my grandmother's hush-hushed attempts to divorce him; my mother's blistering lifetime anger at her oppressive father. It even lent insight into why she would have so many children of her own trying to right that wrong and caulk the hole that loss left.

I know about family secrets. Protocol of days gone by allowed for them. The myth soon became reality. And perhaps for both of them, it was easier to believe Georgie was dead.

CHAPTER III
THE WAY WE WERE

UNTIL SOMEONE LOSES AN EYE

It's all fun and games until someone loses an eye. My mother used to recite that to us as children when our roughhousing escalated to frenzied proportions. What did she think we were playing with? Switchblades? Pitchforks? Spears?

Does anyone have any idea what that statement is supposed to be, anyway? A warning? A prophecy? A threat? A joke?

Funny thing is that other mothers were saying that same warning back then. It seems to have been the precautionary mantra of the 60s. Let it be known though that my mother was not one to blindly follow the crowd. She had to add her own nuance. So she would continue, just to make the cheese more binding, "And when that happens, don't coming running to me." Great. If indeed one of us actually had an eyeball hanging out of our heads, we'd have to fend for ourselves on top of it.

Sometimes I wondered if my mother would have been secretly satisfied if one of us made her prediction come true. Not that she would be actually happy that we were down to one eye, but there must have been some parental smugness in being right. A little of the 'I-told-you-so' mentality that comes from rearing seven children. It catapults one to the status of oracle of motherly wisdom.

When my mom used to issue her official edict, it did give us cause for pause, for we did indeed know someone who had lost an eye. My parent's friend lived across the street with his wife and family of four children. But there were only 11 real eyes between them. One of his—the right one I think—was a fake; a fact my older brother disclosed to me ominously. He embellished the story with flourish. "And he has a couple of fake eyes, in fact," said this instant knower-of-all-things-prosthetic. "One of them has a tiny American flag in the pupil which he puts in only for the 4th of July."

While mildly creeped-out by the idea, I have to admit I was intrigued. How patriotic! From that day on, each Independence Day I longed for him to come over so I could peer into his eyeball to find the miniature stars-and-stripes. But this brought up another question: Didn't his mother warn him about the nasty consequences of horseplay run afoul?

Well, I made it through childhood, despite my four brothers and two sisters, with my two eyeballs intact. Thank God. Even with all that conditioning, I have to admit, it has never dawned on me to issue the same ominous prophecy, even when the roughhousing gets violent.

But you might say when it comes to parenting, it's doubtful that my mother and I would have seen eye-to-eye.

THE FRONT SEAT

If the meek shall inherit the earth, the weak shall inherit the front seat, or at least a window. It's a simple truth and the way it was when I was growing up. I had several siblings who had weak constitutions and a predisposition for carsickness. So when it came to car trips, it was they, the weak of stomach, who claimed the best seats in the car.

This was no small matter because we drove everywhere. There were multiple trips to New York, the Cape, and across the Midwest, always by car, never mass transit, and certainly not by plane.

"Can't I sit by the window, please! Just this once?"

"You know your sister gets car sick. She needs to sit by the window."

Being blessed with a strong stomach was a curse. It sequestered me to the back seat, wedged between two smoldering bile Vesuviuses, apt to erupt at any moment. One quick turn, one humid day, one bad jolt, and it could all be over. Or be all over. Let me say, there is little comfort traveling to Nebraska, knowing that the people flanking you are constantly fighting the urge to puke.

But to this day, what I have never understood is the supposed antidote: the need to sit by the window or, even more plum, the front seat. Remember those were the days when kids were allowed to sit in the front seat. Cars were meant to be stuffed with as many bodies as humanly possible because these were the days before safety. The days before seat belt restrictions and airbags—the days when families of five were considered small.

So I spent my childhood seeing America over the tops of my siblings' heads, keeping a constant prayer vigil that they could keep a cap on things. During these trips, it helped to keep a watchful eye for the first signs that things were going awry. Ghastly pale complexion, a rolling back of the head, shallow, raspy breathing. A weak call for help, and possibly a dropping of the head between the knees. Watching this misery, I rued the days I actually wished carsickness on myself, greedily desiring all the great privileges that went with it. It just wasn't worth it.

And strangely now, as an aging sturdy-stomached adult, I see how the patterning of my youth has influenced my own traveling options. When I encounter someone who struggles with motion sickness, I am the first one to ply them with pills. I also prefer to fly. Everywhere. Even down the street. Oddly, when I do fly, I don't ask for the window or the aisle. I am one of the few people I know who opts for the middle seat. I guess it just feels right. There is something comforting knowing that I am out of the line of direct fire.

SIXTH SENSE

Like most other families, mine had many legends and favorite stories. By far the fav, was the one about my older brother. When he was born, he had six toes on his left foot—eleven altogether. My mother's own explanation of this abnormality just proved to add spice to this legend. She truly believed she was meant to have twins, and this sixth toe was obviously some genetic reconfiguration of my brother's twin. Or, rather, all that was left of his twin. When my brother was a few months old, he was carted back to the hospital where the toe was surgically removed, and plopped in a jar of formaldehyde for later study.

To make matters worse, in what seemed like an unforgivable act of negligence, my mother left the hospital toting my brother sans his toe. Upon her every recount of the story, we would burst in outrage at this act of abandonment. After all, it was my brother's toe, and rightfully ours. To make the situation almost unbearable, no one could produce a photo of the six-digited hoof, though we were assured that several were snapped. How could you misplace such a treasure?

The story was so fantastic in and of itself, but was lacking a visual, either on or off the foot. I, like others who had a little P.T. Barnum inside, saw fame and fortune in that toe. So it came to pass, with every telling, that the story evolved into one of mystery, curiosity and outrage. With just the right amount of panache in the telling, the story would beg the same question: "Why did they have to cut it off?" It would have been infinitely better, and more profitable, for us to have a brother with a sixth intact toe.

I used to think a lot about that toe. I often envisioned the toe suspended peacefully in the bell jar of strong smelling-fluid, like some fetal pig, turning all whitish and wrinkly. The toe in my fantasy had a tiny, little toenail, and—thanks to my mother's twin theory—if you looked real hard you could see the miniscule features of a face on it. It was identical to that of my brother's. I always felt sorry for his diminutive twin who would be destined to float in a jar forever.

Years passed, and I all but forgot about the toe. Then my brother's son was born. The little tike didn't have six toes on his left foot; he had six toes on both feet. And of course, they were surgically removed. What is it they say about history repeating itself?

ODE TO RAGGEDY

I cleaned out the attic last weekend. It took me two days. But among the various asundry usual clutter, I found among other things my treasured valuables: my college diploma crushed flat at the bottom of a box, 46 tons of old baby clothes, a suitcase of sepia tone photos dating back to the Romans of people that no one is alive to identify, and…what's this? My old Raggedy Ann doll.

The poor doll really lived up to her name now. I picked her up and the remaining bits of her cloth skin gave way under my grasp. She had not aged well at all. But who would? The poor thing suffered the wrath of my childhood, having had her red yarny locks scalped carelessly from her head in a raid on my room by my heinous brothers. Her arms had been stitched and re-stitched so many times, the connective fabric was worn through. After losing her legs in one memorable fight, my grandmother had inadvertently sewn them back on the wrong way, so she was forever pigeon-toed. And her head lolled pathetically to one side, having been severed by the same band of scalawags. A pair of ripped little girl's underwear circa 1960 were pinned around her scrawny waist but her little red painted heart still read 'I love you.'

I threw her away. I know, I know, that sounds bad. But I read the "Velveteen Rabbit," and somewhere in my life I believe Raggedy is alive and running a B&B with Barbie and Mrs. Beasley—hopefully with a nicer wardrobe than I could provide.

But I didn't throw everything out. I saved my favorite greeting card. It reads: "MY GYNECOLOGIST LAUGHED HYSTERICALLY WHEN I TOLD HIM I SUFFERED FROM PMS." You flip the card open: "SO I SHOT HIM." That card was purchased in the hey-day of my militant phase, which I have yet to grow out of.

Back then, males offensively referred to PMS as 'that time of month.' It seemed no matter what legitimately provoked your ire, it was always laughingly trivialized to one, simple, degrading statement: "Aw, it's just that time of the month." Implied therein: ignore her, dismiss her, pay her no never mind, just keep on walking.

Just another glaring example of the crucial lack of understanding that exists between genders. What woman hasn't been sarcastically reduced to the likes of a blithering ninny for complaining about a run in her stockings, a broken fingernail nail and a crummy haircut?

As I finished getting rid of bag-after-box of junk from the attic, I neatly tucked the greeting card away for future use. And thought briefly of Raggedy Ann. She never once complained about the endless torture that was her life. Why? She knew what they'd say. "Aw, it's just that time of the month."

DON'T HOLD YOUR BREATH

If we could pick an age to go back to, I would pick nine. In my dimming memory, it replays like a "Little House on the Prairie" re-run. Nine seems to be the last real year of innocence, the crossing point between naiveté and contamination. Puberty was still at bay, with its frightening trappings of bras, sanitary napkins and—ugh— boy fixation. And it was the year I spent a glorious moment basking in the glow of accomplishment.

Growing up wedged between four brothers one develops a tainted view of the definition of a sterling character. Virtues like valor, truth and perseverance pale in comparison to more measurable feats, like how far you can spit, how loudly you can burp, or what joint of your body you can cup with your hand to make a farting noise. The inability to do any of these things slapped you with the most derisive insult of all—being called "a girl." It was a double shot of shame, straight up.

So being at the obvious disadvantage of actually being a girl, I had to find other ways to impress my male coterie. I had a pretty impressive spitting range and could belch on demand. Sadly, the bright yellow stripe down my back was ever visible in the endless games of Hide n' Seek, or our version, which was known as war. It was a three-way war between Germany, the US and Japan, with teams competing to find each other's hiding places, and the captives sent to prison camp in the garage. I spent a lot of time in the garage, because I couldn't stand the pressure of hiding in the trenches. "You are such a girl!"

But one day, quite by accident, I found I could hold my breath— for a really long time. Almost four entire lengths of the swimming pool, or, in terms of our personal family endurance test, for the entire length of Mountain Grove Cemetery, which extends almost the entire length of one long street, with a stop sign. And there was no cheating either—no secret breathing at the stop sign, just fingers clamped on nose, mouth tightly shut, lungs burning, and face blue as the sky in a Claritan commercial. I was impressive. And it won me for a short while, true male sibling admiration, if not a little brain damage. It ended when my older brother made the swim team.

At a recent job interview, when asked about my many accomplishments, I listed my well-over-a-minute breath-holding feat, but I didn't bother getting into how I can also wiggle my ears, curl my tongue, do the Spock finger-split with both hands (live long and prosper, baby). I figured: best not to brag.

SISTER MARY DENISE

Sister Mary Denise died last week. And with her, so did part of my childhood. Like other good Catholic students raised in these parts, the good sisters who devoted their lives as brides of Jesus Christ shaped much of my scholastic youth. And have also given me much column fodder.

I've tried to figure out how many students she must have taught in her 33-year career. It had to be in the thousands. I along with my siblings were among them. Sister Denise stands out like a dynasty. Her booming voice, her quick definitive stride, and the swish of her white folds were enough to strike fear in the hearts of even middle-aged men. At my mother's funeral, Sister whipped into the church to pay respects. She walked pointedly to the front row where we were all sitting. Instantly, my grown-up brothers popped to their feet in uniform stiffness. She stared up at them and spoke to them in a low monotone. They shifted nervously on their feet, looking to the ground and murmuring "yes, Sister" as they did decades before when they often found themselves on the other side of the law.

Sister was 86 when she died. I thought she was 86 when I had her for English 30 years ago. But every time I would see her, years after I graduated, she hadn't changed a lick. Still pushing that loose lock of gray-white hair up under the black bonnet of her habit. Still stuffing a little white tissue into her sleeve after vigorously blowing and wiping her nose. Still laughing boisterously at her own jokes. Still driven to wet eyes by a good rendition of "Make me a channel of your Peace."

And still quick with the ever-stinging remark to remind you who you are. I remember one Christmas, Gene O'Neill and I went to midnight mass. Fresh and punky in our college years, we were cheeky enough to have a few adult beverages beforehand. As we slunk into the back of the church, we spied Sister Denise, sailing up and down the aisles, her black cloak billowing behind her like a Superhero for Christ. Trapped in her radar, she stopped directly in front of us and nodded approval at our presence. Gene, emboldened by the scotch, belted out, "A very merry Christmas to you, Sister." Her eyes narrowed. As she turned away from us, she looked skyward, and murmured just loud enough for us to hear, "Jesus, Mary and Joseph, pray for us."

Sister Mary Denise died last week. And whether it be honing the vital ability to diagram a sentence, developing an inner sense of morality, or just copping a genuine dislike for authority, for those who ever claimed her as their teacher, it is highly doubtful she will ever be forgotten.

MY MOTHER, THE JEW

Schlemiel, schlemazel, hasenpfeffer incorporated.

Remember that show "Laverne and Shirley"? Ever wonder what that meant? It's Yiddish with a little German thrown in. Literally, it means, "Dope, unlucky person, rabbit stew incorporated." Another one of life's mysteries solved.

As far as I'm concerned, if I could learn another language to help me get around in this global community, it would be Yiddish. My mother was a Jew—trapped in a Catholic dogma. Actually, she just acted like your stereotypical Jewish mother, right down to the chicken soup, Jewish penicillin. She had the chutzpah to sprinkle Yiddish expressions throughout her conversation like paprika over deviled eggs. "You want to nosh?" "I like to kibbitz." "I don't need to hear the whole megila." "That poor schleimel—he is such a klutz." "That dress makes your tuchis look like the state of Rhode Island."

Raised Catholic by a woman who spoke Yiddish—no wonder I'm

confused. So confused that I confuse other people. For most of my life, people assumed I was Jewish. A boy once dated me in college, I later found out, for the sole reason he thought I was Jewish. He didn't know I was a shiksa. How facacta.

Although it is not a national language, Yiddish arose (c.1100) out of a blend of a number of German dialects in the ghettos of Central Europe, and from there it spread to other parts of the world. Its vocabulary is basically German, but it has been enlarged by borrowing from Hebrew, Slavic, Romance languages, and English. Basically, it's like learning a half dozen languages in one. Talk about a value. Oy vey.

Yiddish is such an appealing tongue because it feels like you are eating the expressions. They roll around in your mouth and have a texture all their own. Best of all, they sound like they mean. Very onomatopoeia.

As I said, I am not Jewish, but some of my best friends are. In fact, it was thanks to my colleague and pal Barbara, who was like a shvester to me, that I learned more about Yiddish expressions than if she were my melamed. She never kvetched. If I was wearing a shamatah dress, she would tell me. Some shmutz on my face? She would wipe it off. If I were feeling shpilkes before a big interview, she was there to hold my hand. If she had been a man, she would have been a mensch.

Feeling a little farklempt? Who could blame you. You probably needed to read this like you needed a loch in kop. Maybe I could become an honorary Jew. But I'll leave it alone. For now, let's just say 'Zay gezunt.'

(Answer Key: chutzpah—nerve, facacta—ridiculous, farklempt—confused, kvetch—complainer, kibbitz—meddle, loch in kop—hole in the head, megilla—whole story, melamed—teacher, mensch—nice gentleman, nosh—eat a little something, schlemiel—dope, schlemazel—unlucky person, schmutz—dirt, shiksa—a non-Jewish girl, shamatah—rag, shpilkes—nervous energy, shvester—sister, tuchis—butt, zay gezunt—stay well, goodbye)

THE KID WHO WET HER PANTS

Ever wonder what happened to that happy band of misfits you hooked up with in kindergarten? For some reason, those kids made a fundamental impact on my life. Even me of little memory has a vivid memory of my first day of school, when Miss Mazda—a copious woman with large arms and a wonderful comforting nature—took me by the hand after my father and grandfather dropped me off. There I was in my little red jumper and Buster Browns, launched into my first foray into the world around me, complete with its oddities.

I felt very small that day, as my dad handed me off to the largest that was Miss Mazda. He patted me on the head and my grandfather grunted, and off they went. I fought back the tears as she took my hand and toted me around the room, calling out orders to the milling groups of other four and five year olds. Another girl named Ann gripped her right hand, a girl completely comfortable in her new digs. She was the antithesis of timid. Very animated, just chattering away, speaking aimlessly to the air around her. Overtime, I would learn that Ann's endless prattle was her trademark and her curse. We didn't have ADD back then, so she was just considered having a 'short attention span.'

Then there was Denise, the girl with the perennial bloody nose. The continual hemorrhaging made her always sound like she had a stuffy nose. Like clockwork, at least twice a week during naptime, it would suddenly erupt. "Mith Mathda," she would quietly utter. The poor kid would gingerly make her way forward to the front of the classroom, head tilted way back, feeling along like Helen Keller through the large tables on which we laid our heads.

Little Tommy Y. thankfully was never seated at my table. The lad could have been the poster child for the unwashed masses. His face had a dirty tinge to it, and he had ink stains around his mouth, fingers and God knows where else. This was particularly mysterious because we weren't allowed to use pens, making him suspect of concealing a contraband ballpoint. To make matters worse, he had a moony crush on me that made me want to punch him—hard. As my mother would say, "That boy needs a good scrubbing."

Looking back I wonder what happened to that odd lot of kids. No doubt, poor Miss Mazda, who was on the fast track to heart disease, is no longer with us. I ponder if Ann ever shut up, or at least found Ritalin. Was Denise able to live a life without cotton stuffed in her nostrils? Did little Tommy Y. finally meet up with a washcloth or a fist?

And I wonder if they ever ponder the fate of the girl who wet her pants?

GRANDMA'S BEST PAST LIFE

Someone I know speaks of past lives but he's not speaking of the spiritual world. It's a reference to all the lives we live in this single lifetime. I now understand this concept perhaps because I am old enough to actually have some past lives myself, and in looking back on what was, they do feel like past lives.

The best advice I ever got was from my mother's mother. My grandmother was a smoker. But all during my childhood she forever warned me: Never start smoking. Seeing the apparent hypocrisy of her wisdom, I once broached her with my 12-year old seriousness as to why she smoked.

She thought for awhile, the single, white cig dangling from her closed lips. I waited. Then she began. It was a story about a young woman whom I had never met. A woman that was she in a past life. Unmarried and in her 20's, this gal worked for a living, typing book-keeping entries for a beer company called Budweiser before Prohibition. She giggled as she spoke of the roaring 20s and the advent of cars and radio. I remained speechless as she spoke of this carefree young woman who danced around the fringe of the speak easy world of New York in flapper garb and short bobbed hair, who sang "I'm just wild about Harry" as she kicked up her legs. She'd sip on tall glasses of pilsner. And she picked up the nastiest of habits—smoking. "I was young," she said as she drew the last smoke out of her butt and ground it into the ashtray. "You know how that is."

Well, yes, I did know how it was—I was only 12. But I had no idea what she was talking about because I had nothing else to compare it to. Nevertheless, I was in shock. Sitting before me was my grandmother, a woman whom had always seemed old to me. She was shy, meek and retiring. There was a strangeness to thinking that this sweet woman who sat at our kitchen table winding bits of string into ever-growing balls, gluing broken dishware and drinking instant coffee—had been another person in what was clearly another life and time. My old grandma, who bore my mother and lived a seemingly mundane existence with my grandfather, was once a high-stepping, beer-sipping flapper.

While she must have known that I couldn't really understand her past thanks to my current entrenchment in her very present, she still often shared with me stories of that happy life that was no longer hers. When she was admitted to the hospital for triple bypass surgery, she was forced to give up smoking after 50 years. At the time, I remember feeling oddly sad about this. That heinous, dangling cig was the only remaining remnant of what clearly was her best past life.

SOAP DISH

My father's first brush with the surreal world of soap operas came in 1971. It was the day that all of us realized the line between fact and fiction has definitely blurred. Our favorite character on the then-relatively new soap opera *All My Children* was shot down over Vietnam. My siblings and I had been introduced to the soap courtesy of my mother and grandmother. During that half-hour, we were engrossed in the ultra-dramatic lives of these make-believe people. So much so, that the day this particular episode aired, we were stunned. It was as if someone we actually grew to know was now dead in the jungles of Southeast Asia. The tragic part was that he was leaving behind the love of his life and unborn child. It was simply devastating.

That night when my father came into the kitchen after work, my baby brother who was then little more than a toddler, came racing in, shouting loudly. He tugged on my father's coat sleeve. "Phil's dead!" he proclaimed, with the satisfaction of someone who had successfully imparted grave information swiftly.

My father went pale. "Oh my God," he said, setting down his briefcase, his mind racing wildly. He paused and looked around. "Who's Phil?"

This marked a new era in my young life. While my mother and grandmother weren't really soap opera addicted, they did enjoy keeping up on the comings and goings of tiny, yet influential, Pine Valley.

I, however, was not so lucky. My addictive nature in full fever pitch by the time I entered high school, I managed to somehow watch all the soap operas. And I do mean all. In addition to ABC, I soon ventured to NBC and CBS, realizing that if I switched stations quickly during commercials, I could conceivably get the gist of almost every soap opera on the air, from Guiding Light to Ryan's Hope and Secret Storm. At one point, I was actively engaged in the story lines of eight soaps.

Mesmerized, I watched as people fell in and out of love (and bed) with each other. There were plenty of folks coming back from the dead and recurring plots of murder and revenge. The fundamental ingredients included star-crossed lovers, lots of lies and misunderstanding, and at least one really, really bad guy and gal.

Adulthood has brought a more sobering attitude toward soap opera watching. With my mother and grandmother gone, keeping up on the happenings in PV just isn't as fun anymore. But I haven't lost my touch. I can turn on any episode and pretty much figure out what's going on.

And the soaps will forever hold a tender spot in my heart. For as I look back on those early years of my life, there was nothing quite as traumatic as the day Phil died.

GO FISH

They say a bad day of fishing is better than a good day at work. Fishing is an enigma. While I don't claim to understand the motivation behind every leisure pastime, I do get the point behind sports and hobbies that require physical exertion, tests of accuracy and skill and endurance. Some would argue that fishing meets the standard for all three. Since I come from a family of fishermen—a long line of them—I have heard it often. There is nothing better in the world than fishing. I have found that golf and chocolate can inspire those feelings, too.

From what I remember of my grandfather, a quiet man, he loved two things. One was baseball—he played infield for a local Midwest team. The other was fishing. He passed along that passion to his progeny, albeit it skipped a generation with my dad and another with me. I never did care for the sport, hobby, pastime, obsession, whatever you choose to call it. But many of my siblings do. And for at least one of my brothers, it is the latter. He could fish 24/7. It is not uncommon for him to engage in a midnight jaunt out to some remote fishing spot off the coast where a school of large something-or-anothers were spotted. He buys boats like Whimpy bought hamburgers, and he will gladly pay you Tuesday for a fishing boat today. He is a fanatic.

I find fishing boring. (I know I am holding a lightning rod in my hand to actually put this in print.) It's just not goal-oriented enough for me. The best I ever did when fishing was on Cape Cod as a kid. Lollipop in my mouth, hair tied back in pigtails, I held a line in the surf and pulled one puffer fish after another onto the sand. I was thrilled. Once on the beach, they'd swell up like the legs of a bride, nine months pregnant. My older brother burst my bubble. "You can't eat those. They aren't worth anything." Then why in the world are we doing this?

You would think that the goal would be to catch the most, or the largest, or the best fish out there. But it doesn't seem to be. One fishing trip after another, my brothers would come in, flush from the elements and laughing. On one such occasion, I asked where were the fish? Oh, we threw them back. Or, we didn't catch anything, really. No fruits for all that labor? "Then how could it have been fun?" I gasped.

My younger brother looked at me as if I had just told him I was really a man. "Fun? Do you think the only thing that makes fishing fun is catching something? No wonder you don't get it." Then it dawned on me. Fishing must be like shopping.

SEATBELT SAFETY

My dad is proud to say that he grew up in Nebraska, and even prouder that he never moved back. But that's not to say he didn't visit. Every summer when I was a wee one, we would take a road trip to visit my grandparents. It was long ago and far away, in time when basic safety precautions like seat belts were stuffed into the seat. How else could you pile five kids, one very pregnant woman and a driver in a five-seater sedan, even if it was American made?

In the front seat was this flip-down arm rest that separated my dad—the man who could steer a car with just his knees—and the passenger—usually my older brother known as "the navigator," or older sister or mother who claimed the front seat mystically warded off car sickness. I was too small to have any rights, so if I wanted a bird's-eye view of endless Iowa cornfields, I had to be creative. That meant the pull-down arm rest, which my dad, ever the safety conscious motorist, agreed would be perfect for my tiny tuckus.

There I would sit, in between stops at local truck stops for meals, busily playing with my Colorforms or trying mightily to create more than just straight lines with my Etch-a-Sketch, nary a thought that I was perched in the death seat. While we never wore safety belts, my mother would insist my sister and I wear matching dresses, fishnet tights, and patent leather shoes, even though we spent 98 percent of the time in the car being seen only by each other and the occasional truck driver.

When my dad grew tired of being crowded, I was sequestered to the back with my little brothers. We would play with the seat belts, cinching them as tight as possible around our waists to see if we could wedge ourselves into the crease of the backseat. I guess we thought it was fun.

Looking back on those days, I am horrified when I think what might have happened being perched so precariously in the death seat.

When my son was born, I took my responsibility for his safety a little manically, and made sure he understood the importance of sitting in a car seat. We had this little ritual. I would chant, "Lean back, arms up." He would dutifully raise his little arms and put his head back so I could maneuver the straps and restraining arm about him. He was then safe from harm.

Lo' and behold one day, I was driving and took a sharp turn. I heard a frantic little voice from behind. "Lean back, arms up, lean back, arms up!" I glanced back. The car seat was flopped over on its side. I had neglected to strap it in place with the seat belt. It was my son's version of, "May Day, May Day." So much for keeping him out of harm's way.

I guess safety belts work best when you actually use them.

DODGE BALL

Growing up on a quiet street had its advantages. The two houses I call my childhood homes both had that distinction. We played hours of hopscotch right in the middle of the road on chalk scratched asphalt and peddled our Schwinns with nary a worry that a speeding car could bury our little faces into the pavement.

It was no wonder, after spending those early black-and-white memories playing games like Johnny, Johnny, may we cross the ocean?; Red light, green light; and Simon Says, I was ill-prepared for school. I was now in a place where exercise had a name: gym. Darwinism at its finest.

In the name of fairness, our gym teacher tried his hand at games that everyone could supposedly play. Games like Dodge Ball. Now those were the days when corporal punishment was king, and Mr. C— while being a kindly member of the laity—easily turned a blind eye to the obvious: Dodge Ball hurt like the dickens. It also widened the already huge gap between the athletic and the non. Dodge Ball just served as a way to drive home the point, while letting the more physical amongst us let off their aggressions.

Mr. C acquired the largest, red rubber ball known to mankind. His intention was good. He figured the more cumbersome the ball, the harder it would be to throw with any accuracy or force. What he didn't realize—because he was never the poor sucker in the middle of the circle—was that its size also made it much harder to dodge, and its sheer weight would knock you down like a duckpin.

As bad as Dodge Ball was, Red Rover was worse. If you never played this game, consider yourself as having had a happy childhood. Two lines of girls, firmly clasping hands, facing each other like twin Great Walls of China, a good distance a part. The captain yells, "Red rover, red rover send So-and-So over (a girl on the opposing side)." So-and-So then dashes headlong into the opposing line, trying to break through. If successful, she is allowed to go back 'home.' If not, she is now a member of the new side.

At 4' 8" and 80 lbs., I was the weak link. No one would call me over because I wasn't built like a future gym teacher. Except on one occasion. The captain, Laura, was a scrawny, knobby-kneed thing known for her softball prowess. I heard my name called. A joke? Yes, and a painful one at that, as I saw the clasped hands toward which I was hurtling suddenly give way. Laura had given the signal to loosen their grip. I flew through, unable to stop until my shoe caught the pavement and I careened face first and legs akimbo into a game of jump rope.

I have become fond of saying, 'If I knew then what I know now.' I wonder if ole Laura is up for a Red Rover rematch.

THE FLYING NUN

Just to clarify, it's a myth that nuns can fly. I've never seen one and I have been around many in my day. But thanks to a popular 1960's TV series, I spent much of my preteen classroom time with one eye to the skies, wondering if my homeroom teacher might go airborne. Of course, that was silly. She didn't have the right habit. (Sr. Bertrille wore a winged coronet conducive to taking flight.)

Like my mother before me, I was educated primarily by nuns. My mother loved nuns. She wanted to be one, and prayed mightily for 'the calling.' A few years later, it was my father who came a'calling. They wed, and he saddled her with raising a passel of brats. A modern day Maria Von Trapp, except the seven of us couldn't sing and refused to wear lederhosen. She would end up always the mother, never the Mother Superior.

Perhaps it was from her that I got my own fascination with women of the cloth. It was in Sr. Mary Josephine's 2nd grade class at St. Mary's Elementary when I first became drawn to the nun's life. Those were the days when nuns looked like nuns. They wore full habits and moved as if on ball bearings. Swaddled in multiple black skirts and covered from head to toe with nary a peek of hair, they were mysterious. That appealed to my 7-year old mind.

But that was just around Vatican II, which as all Catholics know, ushered in the modern church, and subsequently, unleashed nuns from their voluminous wardrobes and let them come out of the closet, so to speak. Habits got shorter, as did veils. Not only could you see their arms and legs, which were just flesh and blood, you could see their hair. Which blew the myth that they shaved their heads. Not much mystery left.

Quite frankly, it was hard to watch. By the time I reached high school, you couldn't tell a nun from a lay teacher, except by maybe the shoes.

Like my mother, I prayed for the calling, knowing full well that if I actually heard it, I would be first in line to bring back the bolts of black broadcloth. I wanted those long rosary beads to swing at my padded hip while I paced the aisles of fearful children. I wanted a huge habit, with the comfort and sanctity that accompanied it. I also wanted a new name and even tried some on for size. Sr. Mary Mary seemed doubly blessed to me. Or perhaps something in Latin like Sr. Immaculata or, given my penchant for talking non-stop, Sr. Ad Nauseam.

Well, needless to say, I never did get the calling. It's all for the best, I guess. The vows would have been tough as I am not big on obedience or even poverty. Talk about changing habits.

LISTEN TO GRANDMA

"It's a disgusting habit. Never pick it up," she warned as she deftly flicked the ashes from the glowing ember into the heavy cut glass ashtray my mother kept stashed on the second shelf of the pantry for Grandma's sole use. An avid smoker, she would visit us with my grandfather a couple of times a month, suitcase in hand. In her leather handbag, was the cigarette case with the brass clip filled with Pall Malls. My grandfather preferred dime store stogies. They were sequestered behind the closed doors of my sister's room to take care of their smoking needs. And for Lou, Grandma's childhood nickname, a need it was indeed.

Lou, like most smokers I have come to know over the years, had a love-hate relationship with her habit which she would have called an addiction if she had been hip to the vernacular of the decade. Or maybe she just avoided the term in general. She could never bring herself to call my grandfather an alcoholic. He just had a drinking problem.

And so it was that Lou had a smoking problem. For 50 years. It wasn't until she had triple bypass surgery that she gave up the butts. But by then it was kind of too late, in terms of quality of life. A series of debilitating strokes followed and she died a few months later.

None of us ever gave her a hard time for smoking, which was curious behavior for my judgmental family. It was just a fact. Grandma smoked. She wasn't proud of her habit. She never once defended it, claiming it was sheer stupidity that led her to smoke her first cigarette. She never once defended her inability to quit, either. It had seemed to us that she had given up and let her harsh mistress have her way.

I listened to my grandmother's advice because even as a young teen, I had figured out that life lessons are best taught by the fallen, so to speak. This wasn't Sr. Mary Denise preaching to me about the sins of premarital sex, after all. This was a woman I listened to—especially her deep, phlegmy cough. It was an endless hacking that shook her body and went on for so long I thought she would cough up a lung or collapse on the floor unconscious. Carefully, I took in the glamorous nuances smoking added to her life: the yellowed stained skin between her fore- and middle fingers, the harsh smell of toxic chemicals on her breath, the gagging taste of stale smoke on her lips, the neurotic even manic need for a butt, and the countless premature wrinkles around her eyes, as she had a habit of squinting hard when she exhaled.

Thanks to her, even to this nail-biting, neurotic, overanxious teen who was ripe for something to help siphon off the stress, cigs just never seemed appealing. When I see teenagers smoking, for whatever personal reasons, I can't help but think of Lou.

CHAPTER IV
THE SEASONS, THEY GO ROUND AND ROUND

THE FALLING LEAVES

How did it get to be October? Wasn't the first day of school last week? Weren't we just at the beach?

I can't believe it's October. I used to love October. It's a fine month. Not too cold but just cold enough to be considered my favorite word, blustery. A fine blustery month. Its arrival fortold of snow, holidays, Halloween, apple pies and winter vacation. I used to love this month.

I first noticed my love fading a few years ago, when my gas bill took steroids and grew twice its size overnight. Such a delight to see a puny gas bill over the summer months, such a treat. Then the mid-October bill came, and threw me a one-two punch. Ever since then, I've been KO'd. When October arrives with temps in the 60s it fills me with indecision. My thermostat taunts me, like the spider said to the fly, "Will you, won't you, will you won't you, will you won't you turn on the heat?"

Yes, October gives me anxiety now. Along with the chill, it somehow marks the beginning of the end of the year for me. First of all, it officially launches gift season, opening the floodgate to a slew of celebrations for people who had no right being born, married, christened or anything else that requires a gift, so close to the holidays. That includes my own son. What was I thinking? And his birthday party has gotten so blown out of proportion. He has more friends to invite than a small country. The days of picking up a Cookie Puss and a few balloons are long gone.

October also inevitably means Halloween. A seemingly simple holiday in days gone by, Halloween is completely out of control now as well. They should have ghoulish party planners for this holiday. At my house, it involves Academy Award winning-costume making, elaborate porch and window decorations, exasperating debates about the immorality of mischief night, and nagging lectures on diabetes and tooth decay.

Fortunately, Halloween wraps up, and whoops, we're sliding into Thanksgiving. I used to love this holiday when I was young and my mother held the iron reins. Now that she's moved on for a well-deserved rest and the family has families of their own, it's a major feat. The debate is launched right after Halloween about what are we going to eat, when are we going to eat it, where's the stuffing, and who wants to watch football anyway?

It also happens to be in October when that sneaking, underlying fear, like a nasty little mouse, starts gnawing away at the cheese which is my conscience—the frightening realization that my mother-in-law has finished her Christmas shopping.

Did I happen to mention how much I used to love the fall?

CARIBBEAN CHRISTMAS

I think I got sunburned last week when I went shopping for my Christmas tree. Silly me, I forget to pack my sunblock and wide-brimmed beach hat for this annual DECEMBER excursion. Who knew that tepid fifty-degree morning would turn into another winter scorcher.

Okay, I admit it, like most, I was having a little problem adjusting to the change in season this year. I always thought that winter followed autumn. I vaguely remember something that we old timers call snow. While I was scrooging about the lack of cold weather—something I normally complain about once it gets here—it was my sister who turned me around. Off we were, holiday shopping, looking for a couple of bathing suits and sandals, when she suddenly chirped—"I love this weather!" Please, I thought glumly, it's supposed to be cold. She smiled and said, "Look at it this way. Pretend you're in Florida, or the islands."

Well, didn't that just do the trick! What the heck was I complaining about? The weather was gorgeous, even if there were only twenty shopping days left. After all, during my growing up years, my family spent every Christmas in the islands. Heat instead of holly; palm trees, instead of conifers; sand, not snow. Doesn't get much better than that. Who cares if it's Connecticut—known for casinos rather than cruises. Replace that mulled cider with a pitcher of daiquiris, dust off the limbo stick, and presto! You're there. Christmas in the tropics, baby. I feel a song coming on:

Have yourself a balmy little Christmas, let your clothes be light.
Pack away your snowsuit—don't be so uptight!
Braid your hair in cornrows for the Yuletide.
Pass around the rum.
From now on it's sand between your toes—they're not numb!
Here we are—unlike olden days—frozen, chilling days of yore.
Hacking coughs they have gone away,
Pass the Bain d' Soleil, once more.
Through the month, we all will wear our mumuus,
    and bask in the sun.
Say ta-ta to winter, for it's on the run.
And have yourself a sunny little Christmas, mun.

SANTA BABY

Dear Santa:

Just a quick note to say thank you. I know, I know. You're thinking: How could one of Irene's girls be so remiss as to wait thirty some-odd years to write a thank you note? Actually, I apologize for never getting one off to you, but it never occurred to me back then. Maybe I thought you left for Florida on the 26th or something.

Anyway, I am actually writing to thank you for the wonderful gifts you left for my son. Let me tell you – you really scored. Not only did you give him everything he asked for, you went above and beyond, as usual. As a parent on a budget, it certainly takes some of the heat off. My son often has asked me after opening your gifts to him, "What did you get me?" Well, the presents I buy pale in comparison. You've got that magic touch, mister.

Speaking of gifts, I have always wondered what kind've deal you struck with the toy manufacturers. You must be the master negotiator, I mean with corporate mentality being the way it is. Or maybe the elves actually do make everything. Working with polymers and computer chips is a far cry from hammering wooden cars. Talk about retooling.

In closing, I would love to send you something. You know, a little thank you gift from me to you. But try as I may, I couldn't come up with a thing. I mean, what do you get a guy who can literally make everything? I guess this note will have to suffice. I hope this letter gets to you. I am not quite sure where you take up residence in the winter. Though I know you have a penchant for really cold places, I suspect there's a sun worshiper under all that red wool. Hey, let me know. I know a great place in the Caribbean. Very low key, very discreet.

With fondest wishes, Lenore

P.S. I know this is ancient history, but remember back in 1966, when I smacked the next door neighbor's kid with the fence post? There was a reason for that. Kenny was spreading ugly rumors to my little brother about your existence. I was actually defending you. Not like I was being naughty, or anything. Anyway, just thought I should clear that up, seeing as my sister ended up with the Barbie dream house for Christmas last year, even though I asked for it. Hey, but no hard feelings.

'TIS BETTER TO GIVE THAN RECEIVE

"The Grinch hated Christmas! The whole Christmas season! Now, please don't ask why. No one quite knows the reason. It could be that his head wasn't screwed on quite right."

Or it could have been that his presents were a fright. Did anyone think that maybe the Grinch's problem was that he wasn't forgiving about getting the wrong gifts? It seems to me that the favorite thing for people to buy me is clothing. I must either look like a ragamuffin or maybe I just wear the same thing all the time. Don't get me wrong, I like getting a new wardrobe. But buying clothing is tricky. It can be the most thoughtful of gifts, especially when the giftor is truly in tune with the giftee's style and tastes. At the same time, it can be the biggest cop-out gift for the 'get-me-outta-here' giftor, who grabs the first thing off the rack and has it wrapped.

But while others are beating a path to the department stores today, returning unwanted items, outfits that don't fit and clothing in the wrong colors, I will not. They'll be waiting in long lines to exchange all the togs that don't suit their tastes, but I will not. I don't think I would even know how to exchange a gift. No, I will proudly wear those items, clinging to the belief that the giftor who bought me the fuschia tube top with the phrase "Touch of Class" across the chest in metal rivets, was well-meaning. I will do this because that's who I am. A two-faced chicken. I don't want to hurt anyone's feelings. Especially when they're nice enough to buy me something.

This comes from years of training. After all, my mother came from the old school. You know the one where everything left on your plate could easily feed the starving people in [country name goes here.] She raised us to not be ingrates, which—loosely translated—means you should appreciate everything you get, or at the scanty least, just pretend you do. In fact, my family is so good at this—we enthuse to such a degree in our escalating, pretend delight—that the giftor often promises to buy us another one next year. It always backfires on us.

But a strange thing happens when you fake liking things that you don't for over four decades. You get to the point where you cease to know what you like and what you don't. In the long run, this benign confusion makes you a wonderful giftee. You end up liking everything you really hate.

Or maybe you should just go stand in line, and get something you like.

Then the Grinch thought of something he hadn't before! "After Christmas," he thought, "I'll go back to the store." And what happened then? Well in Who-ville they say, that the Grinch's small smile grew three sizes that day!

LAST MINUTE SHOPPER

In a perfect world, holiday gifts are not measured by the pricetag but by the pure joy they bring. Since bypassing commercialism is a moot effort in this country, I think we have all tacitly developed our own philosophies about gift giving.

"I saw this and just knew it was you!" A popular strategy and one I personally like, even though it can be a knife that potentially cuts both ways. Upon unwrapping, I hold the item in my hands and wonder just what it means to be given something that is really me. Yet at some level, whether I like the gift or not, it appeals to me. This theory also goes hand-in-glove with the "I bought you something you would never buy for yourself" philosophy which can also be enlightening.

Then there are the crafty among us who believe that "All holiday gifts should be homemade." I will tell you flatly: this is a bad theory, unless you are fully in touch with your inner Martha. I give you my sister-in-law, replete with torrid images of her four children chained to the craft table, cranking out gifts. "Faster, faster," she yells. The bottom line: at the end of the day, there's just so much you can do with a Clorox bottle bird feeder.

There are a surprisingly large number of people who just hate giving gifts, ascribing to the "Oh well, I've got to get her something" theory. They grumble about crowds, whine about money; give no thought to anything and buy the first thing they see. Ironically, these gifts are often really good.

But of all the gift giving philosophies in the world, the one that takes the cake is that of the subliminal gift giver who ultimately gives you what he really wants. Case in point: My dear friend got married recently. Under her tree on her first Christmas of marital bliss, was a small, expensively wrapped gift. She whipped open the box and inside was an electronic pendant on a nylon cord. It emitted an electronic beep-beep-beep which supposedly bounced off a satellite to pinpoint her whereabouts.

Too new to marriage to yell out, "What the hell is this?" she sucked it up. Her spouse excitedly told her that they were going on an all-expenses paid, survival skiing trip to the wilderness of Montana!

Skiing the backcountry for three solid weeks! And, bless his soul, they were leaving in just a few hours, and she didn't need to pack a thing. Why? Because they would be sleeping in the same clothes they wore during the day. For at the end of their exhaustive eight-to-ten mile daily skiing treks over mountainous terrain using nothing but map and compass, they would be sleeping in unheated, abandoned cabins alongside other lunatics who were doing the same thing.

The electronic pendant? That would help locate her body in the likely event of an avalanche.

HOLIDAY, SHMOLIDAY

It's a solid week after the holidays officially ended and I am still exhausted. Like most people, I have to travel over the holidays. But I'm not just talking about over the road travel. I'm talking about time travel.

I have spent each and every Yuletide of my life, save one, with my entire family. All the siblings and extended family with whom I grew up, the parents and grandparents who raised us—basically the main characters of my own personal Christmas Past.

I don't know about you, but something happens when my family gets together. We revert. Despite all of our efforts to be grown-ups, it eventually comes to pass that one or more of us slips back into an old role. Then it's just a matter of time before the rest of us collapse like a row of dime store dominoes. Before you know it, it's 1969. Time travel. Face it—it's tough traveling back. Tends to take a toll on one.

It often starts with my very mature brothers. There's a synergistic change when there are more than two of them in one room. They get younger. The more of them, the younger they collectively get. Finally, they are reduced to a bunch of preteen brats picking on everyone with childish glee. This of course is all I need to hop my own flight to the sixties. I find myself fighting the desire to go tell on them.

Go tell whom? What's my father going to do? Spank them? Make them do more chores? Wash their mouths out with soap? That's just one of the problems with holiday time travel. There's no recourse for those who don't behave. We're chronologically too old to punish.

In addition to reverting to our younger, more moronic selves, we also tend to talk of the past a lot. Embarrassing stories, mortifying memories, shocking lies—all get rehashed between courses of roast beef and apple pie. It's bad enough they actually happened once. Reliving them for the 30th time is torturous and…hysterical. Maybe it's all that laughter that runs me ragged.

As we fight to be heard over each other and vie for attention, the table talk finally turns to memories of the most important one who's missing—our mother. The laughter turns to quiet. And that childish need to be with her doesn't seem so childish anymore. It seems personal loss has a timeless emptiness all its own.

Of course, the hardest part of time travel is reentering this time zone, this year. My father has to be continually reminded that my sister is indeed old enough to drive and, no, we all don't live together in the old house anymore.

I love the holidays, and I guess I have to admit, I even love going back in time. I'm just thankful I don't get motion sick.

DE-TREE

We finally de-treed the house this weekend. If the airlines can de-plane us and the railroads de-train us, why can't we de-tree? As you know, de-treeing is a very messy process. A month ago, when we first gazed at it with every decoration in place and all the others were oohing and ahhing, I was the one already worrying about the day it had to come down.

That day was Sunday. Despite protest from the others, whining about how unfair it is to deprive the house of this wondrous, wilting conifer, the tree came down. And with it, hours of tedious cleanup.

First, there is the decoration repackaging. I am not one of those people who can name every decoration on the tree and tell you the history. There just aren't many stories attached to my ornaments. And they're a pain to pack. Try as I may, I am no Martha Stewart. It takes meticulous patience and attention to detail to repack bulbs.

I used to keep all the tiny boxes that originally housed the ornaments. But over time, I got them all mixed up, so they often ended up shoved in the wrong boxes. The old family ornaments were easier. They have for years been wrapped in old Butterworth sewing patterns from dresses made long ago by my mother and grandmothers. I religiously continued this tradition, until the patterns were nothing more than tatters. There was some melancholy in putting these dwindling heirlooms away. One or two never seem to make it to the next year. But I take comfort in knowing that at least their hooks stem back to my early childhood.

Second, there is the cleanup. This year, there were more needles on my rug than are blanketing the redwood forest.

Now usually, I would expect this. But this year, it truly came as a complete shock. The constant battle for Christmas tree owners is keeping the tree fresh and perky. I really thought we had it mastered this year. Not only was it nicely shaped, it never shed a single needle in the weeks that it took center stage in our living room. It even passed the needle test—you know, the one when you accidentally brush up against it, and 4,000 needles cling to your sweater or flutter to the floor. I didn't have to haul the vacuum out once to clean up tree shrapnel.

But now I know why. The tree was saving up for its final swan song—giving us its best parting shot. It was basically bald by the time it was finally pushed through the front door. And all those tiny needles, now petrified into tiny swords, were left marking its trail. I know an act of spite when I see one.

I used to balk at the idea of an artificial tree. It's funny how something as small as a pine needle can change an attitude.

SAY GOODBYE TO OLE MAN WINTER

I finally have to admit it. I've known the truth for a very long time, but have so wanted it not to be so. Why? Like most New Englanders, I think I've felt the subtle pressure to just grin and bear it. After all, that's what it's all about, isn't it? I mean, living here in New England is all about the seasons. So how could you be born and bred here and not love one of the main seasons—and reasons—for being here?

Well, I don't love one of the seasons. And it's right around the corner. I am admitting this in the spirit of truth and honesty, which is my New Year's Resolution—unless I try to give up nail biting again or watching reruns of *The Anna Nicole Show*. I do not love winter. I don't even like it a little bit. All that malarkey about winter wonderland and Currier & Ives leaves me as cold as the frozen tundra under my duck boots.

But, like a marriage gone bad, I learned to live with it. Winter and I agreed to coexist on a plane of mutual apathy. It arrived; I prepared. Hauled out the parkas, mitties, mufflers and ugly boots. The sleds for the kids, the tires for the cars and kiss that clean kitchen floor goodbye for at least five months.

As I grew older and wearier, I launched a silent protest to Old Man Winter's expected (never invited) arrival into my life. I began a boycott. Unless absolutely necessary, I stopped spending hard-earned dollars on winter gear. No more new winter coats, gloves, scarves and hats to herald the season. Last year's would do. When a kid grew out boots—here, have mine! I'll just slid old bread bags over my sandals. That'll show Mr. Winter!

Well, it didn't work. Winter kept coming like an unwanted relative at the Christmas feast. But the feelings of resentment have remained and blossomed into what has become, the winter of my discontent.

For my annual Christmas poem, I feel inspired by classic Seuss:

I do not like the winter cold. I do not like it, though I'm told
That winter wears a cloak of white.
But the cold it masks fills me with fright!

It chills my bones, it makes me skid, I do not like winter…
    though once I did.
It used to be a snowball fight, an icy fort. Oh what delight!
But I was young, and loved the cold.
Now I use Retinol A, for I am old.
My skin is thin, my soul, less hearty.
(That's what happens over forty.)
I do not like winter. No, not at all.
Give me the summer, the spring, the fall.
But never winter. To me it's a scam.
Even served up on a platter and smothered in jam.
For I just don't like winter, woosie that I am.

CHRISTMAS LETTER

I often thought it might be fun to send out a bunch of Christmas letters to strangers. You know, just whip through the phone book and do a random mass mailing. For that's pretty much how I feel when I get Christmas letters from people—like my dad's second cousin's daughter—whom I barely know. My letter would read something like this.

Dear Friends:

How time does fly! Happy Holidays to all. We're happy to report that the season finds us hopeful and happy, especially with the news that Herb has moved up on the liver donor's list. He says as soon as he gets a new one, he'll start up at his AA meetings again.

The kids are fine. Jolene is a new person now that she has found Mr. Right. She and Chet live close by, and he seems determined that this is the year he finally lands a job. And Jolene! Well, she is just beaming. It's remarkable what facial wart removal can do for one's self-esteem. I think this fourth marriage will finally stick. Of course, she misses her kids. But their foster parents are princes and send pictures every season.

Buster and Lily are enjoying the good life in sunny California. Happy to report that they are finally out of the woods with that tax evasion mess. The IRS can be such sticklers about detail. It appeared the whole thing was just a matter of a few missing zeroes, nothing that re-mortgaging the house and a few hundred hours of community service couldn't fix.

Mark was released from prison as of August 16th. Living in a confined space for so many years has given him the itch to move around. Who can blame him? Thank God for that P. O. Box in Montana, or we would never find him.

We took our annual trip to Omaha to check on the family plot this fall. Seems we had lost track of Aunt Marge over the last few years, so we decided to swing by her nursing home. At 109, she's alive and kicking. Well, alive anyway.

One sad note: Mr. Sweetums is no longer with us. Rather than go through any type of messy court battle, we agreed to put him down. I still don't think the attack had anything to do with his breeding. There is no evidence that a Pitbull-Rotweiller mix is any more aggressive than a Lab. At least that's what the guard dog company who trained him told us. Anyway, the little kid is fine. They were able to sew his leg back on and he should walk again with the aid of a cane and several months of therapy.

That's about it from here. We love and miss each and every one of you, and hope you'll drop a dime when you have the time.

Love, Us

CHRISTMAS ORPHAN ORNAMENT

It never fails. This happens year after year after year. It will be weeks after the decorations are down and all that's left over from the holiday festivities are a few extra pounds. There, under the sofa, stuffed behind a chair cushion, or wedged in the creases of the dog bed, I'll find it–an orphan ornament. Somehow in the haste of stripping the tree, this solo, glittering remnant of Christmas past has been left behind, as the caravan of bulbs, lights and holiday hoopla long ago made its way out of the living room and into the dark recesses of the cellar for a long winter's nap.

Now what. I sigh. Clearly the last thing I want to do—and therefore the last thing I will be doing—is to go down to the cellar, dig around the crawlspace and drag out the boxes of decorations just so the lone ornament can be in good company.

The question hangs in the air like smog: what do you do with a homeless Christmas decoration? Once again I have to be the one to make the tough decisions. My first thought is to throw it out. It would be the swiftest and simplest solution to solve my immediate dilemma. But my mother, grandmothers and entire ancestral line of thrifty, foil-saving, penny pinchers would never give me a minute's peace. I already sense their cold stares from beyond the grave.

My second thought is to stuff it in the junk drawer, but I might as well just go back to my first thought, as I will have to surely throw it out because it will be quickly shattered. And most likely, my husband will cut his finger on it, begging the terse question: Why was there a Christmas ornament in the junk drawer?

My third thought, and the one I always pick, is to incorporate the lone ornament into an existing piece of my decor, hoping that everyone will think the silk flower arrangement on the dining room table always had a sparkly, gold reindeer perched in between the dried hydrangea and thistle. Which comes to the crux of the matter. The ornament that gets left behind is never one of those innocuous ones that could pass for any season. It's always a shiny Kris Kringle or some gaudy, glittery thing that just screams "Christmas!" In the past, I have been forced to hang elves off of sconces in the dining room, and stick a jovial neon Santa in the soil of a large indoor potted plant. This year, it's a plastic globe filled with fake snow and a little skier boy smiling wildly wearing a Santa hat. He'll be spending this year skiing down the sides of a large porcelain bowl on the buffet.

The sad part to this whole tale is that I then get used to having these decorations year round as part of my decor—a veritable designers nightmare. Soon will come the day when I will have no decorations for the tree—they'll all be hanging around my house.

NEW YEAR'S RESOLUTION

Here's a multiple choice question for you. Please circle one. Will you keep your new year's resolution?

    a) You will try very, very hard.

    b) You will probably mess up.

    c) Other people will probably mess it up for you.

    d) Only if it doesn't have anything to do with quitting bad habits.

    e) There are more important things in life than conviction.

Okay, drop your pencils. If you're like me, this is the hardest time of year—the end. Some people stress over holiday shopping, others over having a house full of family. Me? It's the stress of making my new year's resolution. There is so much riding on it. They say the civilization credited with creating New Year's is the Babylonians. Making a resolution is a reflection of the Babylonians' belief that what a person does on the first day of the new year will have an effect throughout the entire year. Thank goodness I'm American.

Contrary to the Babylonians, I've heard some psychologists reason that making a resolution at the turn of each year is bad for your mental health. After all, based on the stats, success is not in your favor. It's something like 1,000 to one that you won't succeed. So if putting an end to your betting problem is your resolution, I'd say put all your money on not keeping it.

The toughest thing for me is picking something I really, truly want to change and have the stick-to-it-tiveness to follow through. They say the most common resolutions are those involving positive behavior modification, such as, to start exercising, quit smoking, save money, lose weight, eat healthier, get organized, etc. These are the toughest to keep because they often require heavy duty personal changes to be successful. I am guilty of failure on all of these counts (except smoking, because I quit before I began.)

Regardless, each New Year's Eve finds me back in the saddle again. They say the KISS method is best in making and keeping resolutions—namely, keep is simple, stupid. Following this guideline, assuming that I am the one referred to as "stupid," I figured out a few things that I could do this year without having to go through intense psychotherapy.

1) Smile more. This requires the slight pull of a few facial muscles. With practice, it's really quite easy.
2) Turn off the TV. This can be tough, but you'd be amazed at the result—it's called conversation.
3) Say 'thank you' and mean it. All the time. A little harder since the vocal chords are involved, but worth the effort.
4) Don't take myself too seriously. Nobody else does, so why should I?

Even with this list, I am still worried. They say that the odds are against me. Oh, what do they know anyway. Maybe my new resolution is to stop caring what they have to say.

THE IMPORTANCE OF ACORNS

It's all about the acorns. Corpulent and massive in size, falling for at least a month like hailstones, the local acorns are foretelling what weathermen can only guess: an early and hearty winter ahead. And the leaves agree. Fallen, crimson comrades already lie face down on lawns across the county. One glance skyward to the highest branches tells the truer story. Thousands are ready to join them soon, signaling among other things the end of lawn mowing and the start of leaf raking. Another season is upon us and already ready to go.

Nature, while having the bad rap of being wild and unpredictable, is more often than not courteous enough to send its couriers ahead. Whether or not anyone pays attention is debatable. But when it comes to the early arrival of one of the more belligerent seasons, nature does have calling cards. And it has to, for there is no fence-sitting for winter.

Winter is the most decisive of all the seasons and rarely does it wait for permission to arrive. Eschewing a formal invitation, winter lacks the gentility of spring, which silently waits in the wings and pouts until allowed to enter. And that is usually and only when winter is completely spent and ready to relinquish its grasp. And then it just melts away.

Along with acorns, the wooly caterpillar has also been saddled with the responsibility of predicting early winters. And the ground hog is his bookend, supposedly foretelling the end of the coldest season by seeing his shadow.

Most of this is considered folklore of Farmer's Almanac variety but who doesn't hold some credence in old wives tales? Doesn't a double yolk mean good fortune and plentitude? Don't bad things happen in threes? You know you'll never find a 13th floor in a skyscraper. Myths, omens, superstitions, mojo, all have their roots in belief. Organized religions aside, belief is often the complicated, very personal result of living. It's as unique as each individual's host of experiences and interpretations.

Meteorologists say wind often accompanies weather changes. Big wind can indicate big change ahead. Wouldn't it be nice if life, like nature, would send along a predictor or two, a heads up to get our attention before change barreled in? Who wouldn't appreciate a windstorm prognosticator before the rug was about to be pulled out from underneath?

Even though animals, flowers and fauna can predict incoming storms and changes in weather, humans seem to have lost that ability. As Foghorn Leghorn would put it, our collective sixth sense and acute intuition is "bout as sharp as a pound of wet liver." In a world where intuition is pooh-poohed, it seems odd to tell a child to trust his instincts. Going with your gut runs contrary to the generally accepted belief that most decisions should be based on rational thinking and solid logic.

But maybe, just maybe with all this profound over-thinking and deep analysis we have misplaced something much more valuable: our acorns.

CHAPTER V
GROW OLD ALONG WITH ME

ALL GROWED UP

I officially became an adult at 20, as a senior in college. I bought my first sofa. In the vernacular of my waning youthdom one of my college cohorts tied coming of age to purchasing furniture.

"You're an adult when you start acquiring large things," my roommate said. She has since mastered being an adult as she has acquired many, many large things, including a horse farm in Pasadena, an apartment in New York City and lots of oversized cars.

Growing up to me was earmarked by undergarments: not so much when you got to wear a bra, but when you got to wear a girdle. As an under-ten year old, I would watch in awe as my grandmother, my mother and eventually my big sister winced as they pulled the restrictive things up over their lower bodies. (Granted, my sister only wore one in her teens to keep her stockings up.)

I longed for the day I, too, that could wear a girdle and be a grown-up. That day has yet to come. L'Eggs pantyhose took care of that.

At three, my son told me that when were you officially grown up, "you got to wear a gold ring and drink beer." Where did he get that from?

My little nieces like to play dress up, and will often pick the slinkiest outfits from the trunk—often, old satin slips or teddy's—clomp around in gaudy high-heels and boas. "Working tonight, are we?" my little joke lost on them. "No, we're grown-ups." Hmm, who were their role models?

For my younger sister, it was coffee drinking. "Only adults drank coffee. I really felt grownup when I began to order coffee, of course, with tons of cream and sugar."

It's funny how your definition of being a grownup changes as you actually do grow up. All those things that used to be trappings of adulthood then turn into curses and worse yet, habits.

Even in my late 20s, the coffee drinking, beer swilling, sofa-owning adult that I was, I would look at people who were older, more sophisticated, and think, "Wow, I can't wait until I'm an adult." Moving through my 30s and purchasing a whole slew of large things didn't make me feel much like a grown-up: more like a kid who owed her parents (a.k.a, credit card company and the local bank) money.

But I must admit that the one thing that makes me feel grown-up is other people: being called "Ma'am," having friends with kids getting married, hearing the slang of teenagers and really having no clue of what they're saying. That stuff makes me feel like I'm a grownup. Or maybe just old.

It's one of life's cruelest letdowns, folks. You're finally a grownup when you start to feel old.

SCHOOL DAZE

It's not as if I didn't know it was coming. After all, the commercials have been on TV. But when someone asked me the other day, "When does school start?" I admit, I was shocked. School? Already?

It's still summer to me. Plenty of beach days, plenty of long mornings without having to rush people out the door, plenty of time to plan one more day trip. No need to buy yogurt in plastic sleeves or a pricey variety of prepackaged foodstuffs known generically as 'snacks.' I'm one of those who likes summer much more as a parent than I ever did as a kid.

As a kid, it was the idea of summer that was grand. It sort of rolled out lusciously in front of you like an endless, green carpet. But after the first few weeks of mother begging you to 'sleep-in,' even the joy of having no homework wore off and it just seemed rather dull. Sort of like your first prom—you really looked forward to it but in reality, it just wasn't all it was cracked up to be. I was so excited to get back to school. Butterflies would swarm my stomach for a week before.

Now as an adult, summer is grand. It feels great. It's not boring; it's relaxed. There's no stress. No race against the clock, no endless arguments about why school is important, no threats of putting children up for adoption.

And now you're telling me it's over. Why can't denial be a permanent mental condition? I'm not ready for school. The hardest adjustment about the 'going back to school ritual' is the clothes shopping. It's foreign to me. Belonging to the alumni ranks of parochial school kids, we never had to buy school clothes. They were bought for us. And the single trip took all of one morning to the only store in the county that supplied all the parochial and private schools. It was as simple as walking in the door, stating your school's name and dress size.

Presto, a crisp woolen plaid uniform was presented to you. Nothing like the feel of itchy wool in the first hot weeks of September. When mother was feeling generous she actually sprang for a new pair of navy blue knee socks.

But there was one area where the real you could shine through: shoes. While penny loafers, saddle shoes and Buster Browns pretty much completed the selection, it was choice nonetheless. And when all you get to control in your wardrobe for 12 years is your shoes, you'd be amazed at how important they become. I attribute my shoe fetish to this and will base my first impressions on shoes. Like Olympia Dukakis said in the movie Steel Magnolias, "The only thing that separates us from the animals is our ability to accessorize."

PERIOD

When I entered the fifth grade, it was rumored that this was the year that we would be told everything. The big secret about becoming a woman was going to be revealed through the sensitive and capable hands of our homeroom teacher.

I wasn't completely clueless. Being one of seven children, my parents never even tried the stork theory on us. I vividly remember my mother's swollen midriff. I distinctly recall when each of my younger siblings was brought home from the hospital. My mother was more than willing to fill in all the details of the labor. She never held back embellishing in graphic detail the thrill of giving birth, complete with screaming and doubling over in pain.

But I was still a little vague on just how she got that way. So when they segregated our class into boys and girls, and ushered us into the AV room located in the school basement, I knew something really important was going to happen. Sister Mary Theodopholus made a brief introduction about the film we were about to see called "Growing up and liking it." A perplexing title, as it never occurred to me that I could grow up and not like it.

The feature depicted a young girl—supposedly our age—and her struggle with something called "menstruation." There were lots of diagrams illustrating the inner workings of the female anatomy and quite a lot of talk about eggs. When our young protagonist got her friend at the end of the flick, her mother produced a beautiful new yellow dress for her as a gift, along with her sanitary napkin belt and a klunky batch of Kotex.

The message was clear: growing up, menstruating and Kotex made for great puberty. As we filed out of the dank AV room, we knew some secret knowledge had been imparted to us. We were somehow transformed. It never occurred to us that while we got the clinical skinny on getting our first periods, they handily skipped the more difficult topic—sex. The nuns knew their limitations.

But the movie didn't exactly prepare me for the onslaught of womanhood. It didn't address that strange, irrepressible urge to choke the life out of someone the week before your friend comes to visit. Or the fact that mere mention of someone having her period will automatically trigger yours. Or the fact that your stomach triples in size and enters the room a few minutes before you do during that time of the month.

So when the wonderful world of womanhood opened its doors to me a few years later, it was heralded by a backache that felt like my uterus was in a vice-grip accompanied by a wild, ravenous desire to eat salt-covered chocolates. I would have much rather had the yellow dress.

BRAIN FART

Ever come out of a store and you can't find your car? If you're like me, the first thing that races through your mind is, "It's been stolen!"

The idea that you could actually have forgotten where you put something as large and as obvious as a car never crosses your mind.

It's true what they say about the eyes being the first to go. Number two is short-term memory. And there's nothing you can do about it. It's like watching a small boat that's broken its mooring. You watch helplessly from the docks as it drifts slowly out to open sea. "Come back, come back," you mutter softly.

The comforting thing is that I know I'm not alone in this. But while it may happen to you once in awhile, it happens to me every single time I go to the store. And believe me, I've tried all the tricks to avoid this.

For instance, I've tried making a mental note to myself to park in the same general area of the parking lot outside of the grocery store. (The grocery store is where my car usually gets stolen, I mean, misplaced. It's a magic parking lot because the car mysteriously re-appears after about seven minutes.) The problem is, while I'm busy plucking cans of Spam off the shelves, I forget which area I parked in. I often have to stop short when exiting the store and ask myself, "Did I pass the boarded up Goodwill or the dollar Chinese restaurant when I came in?" It's all a blank.

I have even tried writing down the exact location of my car when I visit the mall. I'll scratch it on some odd bit of paper in my purse. But when it comes time to retrieve it, I have to rip through the entire purse. And I can never find it. Obviously someone stole it. One time, I spent hours searching through G Yellow Five South, when I was parked at A Blue Eighteen North the whole time.

I often wonder about my future, and think of my father's aunt who is now 107. She can't remember a thing that happened after 1955. I have this vivid picture of myself, sixty odd years from now, sitting in a nursing home. My then-middle-aged son and grandson come to visit. "Gran, what did you do last night?"

"G Yellow Five South."

My son would turn to his grandchild and say, "She must have played bingo."

MARRY ME

I have the strangest experiences when I go to the grocery store. Waiting my turn at the checkout the other day, the woman in front of me had the gall to pick up items without pricetags on them. "Price check at register 12, price check at register 12." During the wait, I kept myself busy, stacking canned goods into gravity defying structures, and eavesdropping on the conversations around me.

I always seem to shop on the day that social security checks arrive. The fellow behind me, a spry little elderly man, was having a conversation with the old fellow behind him. They were discussing Bob, who I surmised was a mutual friend.

"You know Bob turned 87 yesterday, you know."

"Yeah, I know. You know, he told me he's going to give up his driver's license."

Good for him, I thought to myself, carefully rearranging the oranges by size.

"I know. You know he told me that he just felt he was getting too old to drive."

They broke into peals of chuckles. What's so funny, I wondered, as I lined up the frozen vegetable boxes in perfect uniformity, all facing the same way, bar codes up.

The first old guy laughed again. "Imagine that. Bob thinking that he's getting old."

Laughter all over again. The second old guy then said, "How old are you now anyway? You still in your eighties?"

The first guy laughed. "Hell, no. I'm older than you! I'm going to be ninety four."

Bang! The eleven cans of tuna I had been tediously stacking into a three dimensional pyramid, crashed down on the checkout counter. Ninety what?! I scrambled to gather up the runaway cans. The first guy, who was right behind me, scooped a can up from the floor and placed it on the counter.

"You eat all this healthy stuff?" He waved his hand at my neatly stacked groceries, deftly separated by size, color and weight.

I nodded.

"You know, I like a girl who eats healthy," he gave a little wink, and moved closer.

I chuckled, mildly sickened. He laughed, too.

"You want to marry me? I sure could use a wife who cooks healthy," he said, looking boldly into my eyes, "and has a lot of stamina," he winked again. Dear Lord, I thought, my face turning red. I'm being hit on by a ninety-somethingth. And for the first time in my life, you know, I had no idea what to say.

DEAF AS A DOORNAIL

I got into my car the other day and almost had heart failure. After I put the key in the ignition, the radio blared in my face at such a decibel level, I thought my ears would implode. I quickly clicked it off, and chided myself. "What are you? Deaf?" Only I can talk to myself that way. It seemed strange that I had listened to that outrageous level while I was last driving. The windows must have been bowing to the beat as I tooled around town. All I needed were some low-riders and a wool cap.

It is not without reason that I am concerned. I worry about my hearing because deafness in all of its varying degrees runs in my family. My grandparents were both deaf—excuse me—hard of hearing. My grandfather died in his 60s, but my earliest memories of him were of having to talk loudly to him so he would answer me or at least not ignore me. My grandmother, who lived to a ripe old age, refused a hearing aid even though her doctor strongly advised my father—while she was still middle-aged—that she should learn to lip read.

My grandmother never did learn to lip read. In fact, till the day she passed away, she never accepted the fact that she was almost stone deaf. That's the funny thing about people who are losing their hearing, they don't admit it, which forces you to become part of their denial. You have to change the way you talk to them. It involves amplifying your voice without shouting at them. You have to make your voice bigger, which ain't easy to do when you are nine.

It was a given. When you asked Grandma a question, be prepared for an answer that made no sense. Be prepared to repeat yourself at least four times and have four such answers. Be prepared not to lose your patience and throw up your hands because she doesn't know she's deaf. She thinks you are having trouble speaking. She was the nicest person, too, so it made it doubly hard when you got frustrated.

I often said my grandmother also had the gift of selective hearing. She couldn't hear you if you were two feet in front of her. But if you were in the basement and she was out in the backyard, and you whispered something that you didn't want her to hear, she would hear it. Selective hearing. Or mental telepathy.

Sometimes I feel like I am reliving my youth. My father is also going deaf—excuse me—having a hard time hearing. And it has me worried. My son told me the other day, "You're acting just like Grandpa. You just smiled and nodded at me, but you didn't hear a word I said." Of course, I protested, just like Granny and Dad. I guess the acorn doesn't fall far from the tree.

That's why I am worried.

HAIR TODAY, GONE TOMORROW

All of a sudden, my hair has become a big deal to me. Up until this point, hair has been something that I let my hairdresser worry about. Simply put, I am coif-challenged. I have never been one to use my hair for self-expression. And I don't take too many chances with my appearance. When I walk into a salon, I point to my head and say, "Do whatever you want to this that doesn't require you to be there tomorrow morning to make it look good."

Perhaps that sounds a little lackluster, but at this stage in life, my hair has been with me for over four decades. I am sort've done with it. I've done just about everything humanly possible to it at the recommendation of stylists over the years. Dyed, permed, flat-ironed, teased, twisted, beaded, braided. I pray nightly that bald comes into female vogue, which would make the whole thing a moot point.

No matter what I do to it, lately I feel my head is in a rut. It is in a time warp, stuck somewhere between Diane Sawyer, Martha Stewart and Carol Brady. Nondescript is the adjective I use to describe it. I just don't know what to do with anymore. My mother was a hair purist—never one to tease or spray starch her hair, no beehive for her—she went au natural, and nary did a chemical touch her locks. She loved her dark hair which turned silver around the crown. And she passed down all the myths about aging and hair. You can't have long hair if you are over 40, she would say. I never understood that. The truth is, sure you can have long hair—if you can get your hair to grow long. Mine just peters out somewhere around my shoulders. It seems to just get too tired to keep on growing.

The one thing I always wondered was why so many older women dye their hair blonde. I never understood that, until now. If you continue to cover the gray with one dark color as you age, you start looking like Dick Clark. To make it look natural, it requires that second process—foils, highlights, something to add variation to your hair. It costs money, and doesn't last very long. The easier method is to just dye the whole mop blonde. It covers the gray, automatically adds variation and lasts longer between dye jobs. And no one is the wiser. Except for those who knew you when. And who cares what they think.

Lately, it's a bit disconcerting to see my hair lying on the bathroom floor—little traitors leaping off of a sinking ship. Maybe I'll have my bald wish sooner than I think. Then I'll be the one singing that line from the 60s musical Hair, "Give me your head with hair, long beautiful hair." Or perhaps, Joni Mitchell. "You don't know what you got till it's gone."

DARN YOU

It's happening more and more frequently. I am reminded almost daily that I am turning into my mother. I see her in the way I answer my son, the way I interact with people, her little idiosyncrasies that are also mine, and some of her less attractive personality qualities. I also see her in my siblings, which can be very scary. I wonder as we go through life if our shared experience of 18 years in Skomal family boot camp has permanently imprinted my mother on all of us. I also wonder if the others find that history has begun to repeat itself.

I was an impatient kid. (You might find that hard to believe, given the fact that I have turned into such a calm and serene adult.) But among the many tasks that my mother would ask me to do in my young life, there was one that used to drive me to distraction. It seemed that she could never thread a needle. She could spot a clearance sale a mile down the road, but thread a needle? Forget it. In fact, both my grandmothers also failed miserably at this simple mission, but they had an excuse—they were old. Being the last of a dying breed of seamstresses and obsessive darners it made no sense that these women were virtually blind as bats when it came to handling the tools of their craft.

To add insult to injury, all three wore glasses, too. And all three found them completely useless when it came to the simple task of slipping a piece of thread through the eye of a needle. It was almost comical to watch my mother holding a needle in one hand, thread in the other and trying to judge just where the eye was—all the while, squinting or pulling her head back to see if either motion would help her focus. After multiple tries, completely disgusted, she would call me or one of my other sighted siblings forth. "Get over here. I need your eyes." Of course, I would handily do in three seconds what my mother and grandmothers couldn't do in an hour. Cocksure, I would impatiently demand an answer. "Mom, why can't you do this?" which evoked the inevitable reply, which also doubled as a curse: "Wait till you're my age."

Well, Mom, I didn't even have to wait that long. I can't thread a needle now if my life depended on it. Even with my glasses on. I pull my head back, angle it off to one side, squint, and miss—every single time. That elusive eye of a needle continues to taunt me. I swear it moves on its own. It is the single, most frustrating thing I have encountered in my early stages of aging. Every time I fail, I think of my mother and grandmothers, and feel guilty all over again. But I did learn one thing from them. I never ask my son.

FIT OR PHAT?

I have never once sought out fat in my life, yet it has been unrelenting in its pursuit of me. Try as I may to elude it, it has caught up with me at every turn, and attached itself in the most obvious yet hard to get to places—my upper arms, hind end and, most vulnerable of all, my thighs.

In college there was, and perhaps still is, a phenomenon called the 'freshman ten.' In my case, it was the 'freshman 33 and 1/3.' Blame it on bad coping skills, poor eating habits, stunted growth patterns. Blame it on the pizza man hawking his wares through the dorms after midnight. I met fat for the first time and it has been my faithful companion ever since.

Fat is not the best of friends. It takes up extra space in my pants, keeps me from having a good time at dinner parties and can be a real stick-in-the mud when it comes to health. Ever mindful of it, I work to minimize its presence, pretending it's not really there. And just when I think I've gotten rid of it, the wretch comes back. Fat is sneaky and untrustworthy. It lies. Even those edibles that claim to be fat-free really aren't. Eat enough of them and you'll see what I mean.

The word 'fat' is even considered a vulgar word according to the dictionary. I guess we have to give thanks to modern day linguists—a.k.a. teenagers—who have given the word 'fat' or 'phat' new meaning, one that is synonymous with 'excellent,' 'sweet' and 'choice.' But changing the vernacular does little to change the object. Juliet said it well: What's in a name? That which we call a lipid by any other word would still be onerous.

Fat, even though immensely visible in our culture, is an outcast word. No songs endorsing it have hit the top of the charts, no poetry studied in high school lit classes extol its virtues, no voices rise to the heavens in churches across the land in praise of it. Yet it is such an intimate part of so many of our lives, you'd think it would be more popular.

People dismiss me when I joke about weight issues, as if I don't know what I am talking about. "Oh, you're not fat." Well, I have been fat, I know what fat feels like. As I write this, I know it is just around the bend waiting for me. Fat is a state of mind.

Because I could not stop for fat, it kindly stopped for me.

The scale, it weighed not just myself but mild obesity.

Without the clothes and water weight,

      what's left is what's within.

It's the fat you see, not really me, for I'm really very thin.

BRAIN TO SELF: OUT TO LUNCH

You have reached your brain. Please leave a message after the beep.

I have already admitted that I am memory-challenged. But lately, it seems my brain toys with me just for kicks. In trying to retrieve information, I feel like I'm placing an overseas phone call to a third-world country. On a good day, there's at least a three-second time delay before my brain actually responds. And when it does, the connection is filled with static and hard to understand. I need a digital connection.

To make matters worse, my son has discovered the silly word game "Madlibs," in which you randomly replace parts of speech in a paragraph, rendering the entire thing nonsensical. When you read it aloud, it's so hilarious everyone falls on the floor in peals of laughter with wet pants. At least that's the reaction of a nine-year old boy. The game has been causing problems for me when we make our monthly pilgrimage to the orthodontist to pay homage and give tithing.

There is always a kid's movie playing on the television that hangs suspended from the ceiling in the waiting room. This time, I sat down, and was soon engrossed in pulling lint balls off my coat.

"What's playing?" I looked up. Across from me was a woman, smiling widely. She looked like she could easily eat corn through a chain link fence. No wonder her kid's here, I thought. She pointed to the TV perched above her head.

I glanced at the screen. My mind went blank. "A...a," I stammered, staring up at the animated lions. I had seen this movie at least 40 times. "It's a....a phrase...an adjective and a noun." It was all I could come up with. (Bzzz, bzz, bzz) I was getting nothing but busy signals from my brain.

"Really, really, I know this. It's a...a...," I uttered lamely, moving my hand about in the air for better reception. (Your call will be answered in the order in which it was received.) I was starting to get the letter "m." I was the Amazing Kreskin.

"A movie! It's a movie!" She looked confused. "Disney?" she offered.

"Yes, yes," I leapt up, touching my nose with my forefinger to indicate the right answer. "Which one?" she asked. (Hello? Brain here.) The circuitry reconnected, and the call went through.

"Lion King," I blurted out triumphantly. We both looked relieved.

At that moment, horse woman's daughter came into the room. We nodded our good-byes.

"It was great playing charades with you," she called to me over her shoulder, giggling. The color rose in my cheeks. "Expletive," I muttered to myself, returning to my lint balls.

INTERNAL DIALOGUE

It seems like I always have two conversations going on: the one coming out of my mouth and the one inside my head. It's not something new. I developed my internal dialogue during my childhood when I was encouraged that it was better if I was seen and not heard. But I thought this internal dialogue only happened occasionally. It's a shocking realization to find out that it's going on all the time.

It is doubly shocking to realize that there is a gaping disparity between what my mouth is saying and how I am truly feeling. I remember back when I was in high school. An upperclassmen friend of mine was telling me some sordid—and highly personal—details about her prom night. I clearly remember standing in the hallway, picking at my uniform hem, and nodding nonchalantly, all the while muttering totally nonplussed "uh-huhs" and "oh reallys." Inside my head, however, an eardrum piercing siren was going off as the shy, 14-year-old me reeled from an overload of far too much, not-on-a-need-to-know-basis-type of information.

Except for situations like that, it seems my internal dialogue has been for the most part in the background of my brain—a low murmur of hardly distinguishable thoughts that highly resemble feelings. It was hard to really hear it, so I just ignored it. This continual discourse has, over time, been honed by a myriad of experiences and direct exposure to life's many ups and downs. It has matured and developed a mind of its own, if you will.

And it's getting louder. Apparently, it wants a much bigger audience than little old me. To that end, it's begun to find ways to leak out of my mouth. I think the wall that used to effectively separate the two conversations has developed cracks. Through them, my internal dialogue sputters forth. I often don't even realize it until I see the shocked looks on those around me, and hear comments such as, "I didn't realize you felt so strongly." There I stand, red-faced, wishing I could pull the words out of the air and shove them back into their rightful place.

I hope I am not alone. I remember when my grandmother had her first stroke. It seemed that the wall that shrouded her internal dialogue from the rest of the world, completely collapsed. Perhaps one of the meekest women God placed on this planet, she instantly morphed into a churning mass of opinion if not antagonism. The world finally heard just what she thought of everyone. Her internal dialogue became her external one.

I wonder if that is happening to me. Is it part of the aging process? Is it genetic? I worry about this as I think about those poor souls who stand on street corners launching into major soliloquies to entertain and inform the air around them. I used to callously brand them as nuts, but have begun to rethink my position. What is it that separates me from them, anyway?

My mouth.

COFFEE MUGS

I held the glass in my hand. It took my back to a simpler, albeit immature, time. College. A beery, bleary era, filled with hours of laughter, cheap 16 oz. well drinks for $1.75 and Steak-a-Bobs at a brew pub called Callahan's. Holding the pint glass in my hand, I cradled what once had been a coveted possession. Not many of my peers were able to smuggle a glass out of Callahan's. So prized was this trophy, it sat proudly in my college dorm window for all to see. A status symbol of a neophyte thief.

Now some twenty—ahem—years later, I held the glass in my hand and weighed the question carefully: save or toss?

Toss. Why?

Because I'm a tosser, and that's what tossers do. We toss old possessions away—with some exceptions, of course. The few boxes I choose to carry with me throughout my life are systematically trimmed down each and every time they are moved. I enjoy their memories one more time and then throw them away. The Callahan's glass just didn't make the cut this season. After all, once I'm dead I wonder, who the heck is going to know from Callahan's, even if it was home to the Steak-a-Bob and buck seventy-five cocktail. Off to Goodwill with you, glass from the past.

Being a tosser, I am continually puzzled by the ever-growing collection of coffee mugs in my possession, which I am convinced could outfit a small city. I first ask myself how in the world I ended up with the ugliest, most useless coffee mugs ever manufactured. I think it's because coffee mugs defy the universal law of dishware: the law of inevitability, which states that inevitably, dishes break.

All of them. And it happens systematically according to how much you value each piece.

For instance, your great, great grandmother's sugar bowl, the only surviving member of an extensive 200-piece collection of bone china is bound to fall prey to a well-meaning friend's offer to "help clean up" after the holidays. Smash! You know the sound of dish death when you hear it. One by one, your most treasured glassware becomes extinct in the continual evolution of the species. That is, all except homely, mismatched coffee mugs. They have been granted eternal life—and a home in my cupboard.

My son was recently trying to put away drinking glasses, shoving the tiny nation of coffee mugs in my cupboard around to make room, when one of them tried to commit suicide. It tossed itself off the shelf, nicking the stove on its way down and bounced around on the floor for a minute. It skidded to a halt under the table. The hand of God must have been protecting it. Nary a chip or crack.

In the long run, I guess it's a good thing. When the meek inherit the earth, they'll have something to use for their coffee.

MENOPAUSAL MAMA

Three horrifying things happened to me the other day:

I left a bag of groceries at the store and didn't miss it until I cooked dinner the next day.

I lost my eyeglasses—case and all—and my son, who can't locate his shoes unless they are on his feet, found them.

My father—who has to rely on Post-It notes to remind him to eat breakfast—actually remembered something that I forgot.

It's days like these that get me to thinkin'. Another writer who is a bit older than me suggested that these could be the early warning signs of that time in every woman's life known as menopause. Admittedly, I know little about it. Most of the information I have read never seems to stick, because it pales in comparison to my memories of my mother "going through the change," as it was called then. First of all, it seemed to last forever.

I mean, at least ten years. It was this never-ending, roller coaster of highs and lows. Secondly, everything was blamed on this condition—all erratic behavior, unjust punishment, even blissfully happy moments—everything was colored by the physical status of her spastic hormones. Menopause took plenty of hostages. It was a rough time for everyone, made even rougher because back then it was taboo to talk about it. It was like talking about 'the cancer.' I can still hear my mother half-mouthing/half-whispering that word to her friends, as if saying it out loud made it contagious. Same with menopause (shhh!).

The thought of that event inching ever closer to me is one I do not embrace. Like labor and death, you know it's coming, it ain't going to be fun, and you can read all you want about it, but the bottom line is—you don't know anything until you've gone through it. Then, of course, you're an expert. Too bad with death, you don't have a chance to lord it over everyone.

In order to help deal with this physical anvil hanging over our heads, my friend, who is also an author, came up with the idea that we write a small book about menopause—tongue-in-cheek, funny yet inspirational, light-hearted yet real. Since my best therapy is putting pen-to-paper and my sanity hinges on finding the humor in things, I gave it the go ahead.

One of the things I have found out in the process is that there is a tremendous amount of information about menopause—an information glut, if you will. But oddly, the stigma still remains. Women do not like to discuss it. It's considered a private matter, shrouded by the old Victorian value system that would have labeled you an inconsiderate boor if you dared hint at a woman's age much less talk about womanly issues. Heavens!

Whether that is good or bad is up to interpretation. I still am on the fence about this whole topic. After all, I always err on the side of 'you can never have too much information.' But secretly I ascribe to the axiom 'ignorance is bliss.'

DON'T WORRY, BE HAPPY

"Don't worry, be happy." Bobby McFerrin may have been onto something when his 1988 hit won best song at the Grammy's. At the time, however, I, a cerebral, oh-so-intense twenty-something, thought the ditty was lame. I have since come full circle. I now believe the message is simple but in that, there is absolute truth.

Always one to over think just about everything, I decided to change tactics this upcoming year and actively make things simple. Toward that end, I am adopting this song as my mantra for the new year. It's catchy, written in my range and I can sing it a capella so it makes for good shower serenades.

Lest you think this an easy transition for me, I assure you, it is not. My nickname growing up was "worry wart." My mother used to joke that I was the conscience of the family; that no one else had to worry because I would do it for them. I was the nervous little kid standing by the back door in the morning, coat on, books in hand, waiting for my father to finish breakfast so we could leave for school. I used to mouth silent Hail Mary's through every red light and anguish over the length of time it took to pull into the school parking lot. I had an ongoing fear of being late.

Worry is a drug. And as I grew older, my addiction became a hard core. I was so accustomed to worrying, I went there reflexively, without thought. Though I cognitively understood that worry was a useless activity which only perpetuates the negative not the positive, I found myself unable to stop. It seemed inherent in every new, grand opportunity was the possibility of a multiple of things that could go wrong. And it was my habit to worry about each and every one of them. And, of course, create new ones as well, which is the byproduct of a good dose of worrying.

The problem with that type of systemic worry is that it overshadows the joy of the present. Worry addicts like myself are forced to live in the future because that's where worry thrives best. Always having my feet standing in the present and my head in that which had yet to happen was exhausting. And completely unfulfilling.

As I have aged, reality has been kind to me and shown me that no amount of worry can ward off disappointment or effectively impact the future. Worry is an illusion that I create and while still tempting to dabble in, comes to no personal gain.

While I don't particularly like New Year's resolutions, I do cotton to the idea of making my life better with each passing year. And this year, I will do so by choosing to enjoy the present, knowing that like-begets-like and one joyful, heartfelt moment will hopefully create another and another and another.

"In every life you have some trouble, but when you worry you make it double. Don't worry, be happy."

THE ELEVENTH COMMANDMENT

There was an eleventh commandment our home growing up: Thou shalt not brag. It was as part of our upbringing as spankings and plaid woolen uniforms. Reinforced by the good Dominican nuns, this message was well intentioned and central to the larger belief that bombastic posturing is symptomatic of the larger mortal weaknesses of inflated ego and vain self importance.

While there is truth to this, the lesson seemed to have backfired for several of us in my family, because in general, we have a problem with tooting our own horns. So much so, that each one of us siblings often don't know just how much the others have accomplished because we don't talk about it. Since we are scattered around the planet, there isn't the daily exposure to each other that we once had. It's always a bit of a shock when news comes, word of mouth, of someone's great career milestone.

Part and parcel with the no bragging rule came the unspoken message that what we needed or wanted paled in comparison to the needs and wants of others because that was the definition of selflessness—the polar opposite of selfishness, a sin we were desperate to avoid. This was also underlined and highlighted in our catechism classes, so for us, there was no doubt it had to be true. Sacrifice was good. Fulfillment, consequently, always came with a boatload of guilt.

Now this may not have been the intended result anticipated by my mother or even Sister Mary Denise, but it has been at least for me and several others with which I happen to share a bloodline. And all of these past ghosts converged last week when my sister and I took a trip to the west coast to attend my brother's installation ceremony as a federal magistrate judge, no small dish of peas in the lawyering world.

The trip would have been heartily sanctioned by my mother, because in her mind it would have been the appropriate thing to do. But my mother has been dead for 20 years and while she still manages to control things from the grave, I don't bite anymore. My brother had zero expectation that any of his siblings would be able to swing the long trip in the middle of the work week. I went because I wanted to go. Period. Not because he guilted me, not because I felt I had to represent the family, not because I had some agenda or trumped up belief that I was on a mission. In short, I felt no obligation. I went for purely selfish reasons.

And because I went, I got to see the person my brother has become. During the ceremony, speech after speech about his keen mind, his kind heart and his sterling reputation said everything my brother never shares with any of us because he lives by the eleventh commandment.

Funny thing, at the end of the trip, he was happy, I was happy, and neither of us felt guilty.

CHAPTER VI
RAISING CAIN

NO SLAVE TO FASHION, MY BOY

Am I the only mother of a school-aged kid that didn't buy new clothes for the upcoming semester? It wasn't for lack of trying on my part, believe me. Shopping, even if it is only for the practical school pant, is an activity I would choose over most others any day of the month. And like most shoppers, I have elevated it to an art form.

But this zero-maintenance boy was adamant. Last year's well-worn khakis with the thread strings hanging off the ripped cuffs and a myriad of bland, school-approved shirts were "just fine." And I should be "chill about the whole clothing thing."

With that order, I remain chill and even richer for what he perceives to be his lack of conformity but I view more as his lack of caring. But clearly I am not as chill as him as he coolly saunters through his final year of high school, rumpled in his threadbare clothes and completely at ease with the fact that a hairbrush has never once greeted his locks over the past four years.

The last time my son went clothes shopping with me he was barely 10. I clearly remember the humorous scene: His body draped face-down on the only bench in the store, arms hanging down loosely, his face pressed into the upholstery. The continual chorus, "I hate shopping," rose and fell in muffled tones as he whined his disapproval. No amount of bribery would silence him—not a new toy, ice cream or promise of staying up late. Even the threat of stuffing him a burlap sack and dragging him off to the school for bad boys had no effect. I knew it then: Shopping for my son would always be a solitary experience. So it has come to pass. His look, if you can call it that, is a cross between Good Will chic, Indie band humble and Pee Wee Herman.

It should come as no surprise that in order to fill my maternal shopping longings I have adopted girls throughout my life to shop for and with. Predominately, these have been my nieces who have mothers who hate shopping. I wait for opportunities to snatch them up and drive them to whatever mall or bargain outlet store is within striking distance and we spend the day combing through racks.

My protégé, the oldest niece, has been my shopping companion since she was four and had her own wallet. Carefully, I have imparted my wisdom about bargain hunting and the intricacies of creating a joyous, rewarding shopping experience. I was thrilled when she came to visit this weekend just to shop with her auntie. Of course, my son opted to clean the gutters on the house rather than join his cousin for all the fun.

After we completed our third hour in just one store, she had picked through ever single rack in the junior's department and tried on at least 150 outfits. I wearily realized I had taught her well. She was a pro, now. The legacy lives on and I can die happy.

HOMEWORK HELL

At some point in every parent's life, you go from asking questions to making statements. What used to end in a question mark, now ends in a period or more often, an exclamation point. "Am I a good mother?" "What's wrong with the baby?" "Is it my fault?" give way to the declarative—"Because I said so." "Turn off that TV." "I hope that isn't sass I hear in your voice."

And when you do resort to questions, they are of the rhetorical variety. "Am I speaking to myself here?" "What part of 'no' don't you understand?" "Is everyone trying to make me go insane?"

It seems that all good intention, positive parenting, and perennial validating melts down into one large lump of frustration. I hope this happens to other people. For some, it may be a gradual thing. Usually, they have more than one kid, so it's a process of being worn down over time. For others, it happens all at once. That was me. I do remember waking up one morning and finding to my horror that all my patience was gone. The temper gremlins must have snatched my supply while I was asleep.

I am not proud of the way I turned out. Somewhere along the line, I went from Donna Reed, happily polishing furniture in pearls, to Lizzy Borden, hiding my sharpened ax behind my back. What has taken me from self-reflecting, wonder-mom to frustrated drill sergeant?

It has a name: homework. You know, in my day homework was something we kids did—alone. It was part of our job, like entertaining ourselves, teasing our siblings and back-talking my mother. My mother would no more be involved in my homework than she would be in running my father's company. That was his job. Homework was our job. Bossing everyone around was her job. To ensure that she kept this separation of children and state, she would even shut the door to ensure that we had the quietude to get it done—alone. Homework was only something to be asked about, like health. Anything more than a one-word answer was not required and ran you the risk of them actually becoming interested, or worse yet, offering to help. The one time my father did get involved was when I was in 7th grade. It was an oral report. Sure, it would have been great if I had been standing before the board of directors, but in front of a class of 13-year olds and one Dominican nun, things like puns and ice-breakers, and my dad's sense of humor were lost.

Homework has become a family event that involves everyone. Not that everyone actually does it—it just affects everyone. Tantrums, verbal outbursts, slammed doors, screams of indignation— everyone gets to suffer. Injustice, thy name is homework. And my job as mother has been reduced to one task—making sure it gets done. When my son recently accused me of being a meanie, I calmly told him, "Well, when you're the parent, you can be mean, too."

NORMAN BATES

It was the first day of third grade and this loving mother stuck a sticky note in my son's lunch box. "Remember Mommy loves you." The dopey parenting magazine where I got this bright idea found its way into the recycle bin when later that day I was hotly accused of committing the cardinal sin of embarrassing him. "Never do that again," he warned.

Looking back on this, I have to question my own parenting sanity. Clearly, it was long before I understood the number one lesson in raising boys: Affection is the first thing to go; especially outward signs of it. The less you expect the happier you will be. Hugs and the like for a long time will be on their terms not yours.

It seems in their minds that affection is tantamount to a sick need to baby them. I have been accused of harboring a silent desire to emasculate my son by keeping him tethered to my apron strings against his will to feed this sick need. This, despite efforts to make him do his own laundry, keep his own schedule and cook his own food. This, despite the constant urging to earn his own keep, buy his own gas and keep his own financial records. If he weren't going to college next year, trust me, we would be apartment hunting.

While mommying suffocating him has been the furthest thing from my mind, I often find my pure intent behind expressing love for this child is often relegated to this ulterior motive. As he has grown into semi-adulthood, he has on more than one occasion launched into lectures about how I need to let him go.

Funny, I thought I was doing fairly well with that. Perhaps the biggest mistake I made was letting him watch "Pscyho" years ago. From that day on, I swear, fears of turning into Norman Bates dogged him intermittently. If it weren't so laughable, I would think I must be doing something to feed those concerns.

But the truth of the matter is, while poor Norman had his problems, I think Mrs. Bates had the raw end of that deal. She was dead, for goodness sakes. And I don't relish the thought of having my skeleton strapped to a wheelchair for all eternity while my son dons a wig and pretends to be me.

The Bates family aside, it's been a cognitive and conscious effort on my part to help this kid grow up and away. Though I don't have the heart to tell him this or the apparent chutzpah that he has, the idea of having him live with me, whether I am dead or alive, until he is well into manhood—unless there is a rational reason for it—is more than upsetting to me.

Good byes are never easy. I for one stink at them, but when it is time, as sad as I will be at that moment, I will know that I have done what is right when I finally let little Norman go.

THANK YOU, LADY JUSTICE

Either her boyfriend dumped her or her dog died. I go with the first one, given her apparent youth, relentless weeping and mad texting skills. As she stared down at her cell phone pecking away, tears streamed down her cheeks. Then as an afterthought, she'd glance up and erratically jerk the wheel of her car to keep it from drifting into mine in the left hand lane. In passing her, I gestured for her to pull over and relinquish the middle lane where she was creating quite a logjam of irritated motorists who I might add were not texting. Miraculously, she freed up a third hand and shot me the bird as thanks for my concern.

Like many who share the highways and back roads of this fine county, I have cringed at so many drivers who continue to chat mindlessly into their handheld phones or, worse yet, text while attempting to maintain control of their two ton weapons. Isn't there a law banning this?

It's always nerve racking to see a driver doing two things at once. Though some multi tasking appears relatively harmless—like sipping coffee or sucking on a cigarette—when I stop and think about it, none of it really is. While I don't smoke, I do drink coffee and have done it for over 30 years often while driving. But I do recall a time or two when an unanticipated bump in the asphalt has landed the scalding stuff on my lap or splashed it down my throat in a fiery shot which rendered me momentarily paralyzed at the wheel.

I am not good at multitasking when I drive. I learned this early on years ago while I attempted to apply mascara while driving. After stabbing myself in the eyeball several times, I came to the conclusion that the bathroom—not rearview—mirror is the best place to beautify myself, especially if I don't want to end up looking like Tammy

Faye Baker. When I am driving, I should only be driving.

And I have tried to pass this on to my son. And to that end, I am happy to report, the law has once again stepped in as my parenting aid. My appreciation for the law has soared ever since my son entered puberty. But it truly peaked when he got his Pennsylvania junior driver's license which is issued to those under 18-years of age. This is the greatest gift in the world for a mother of driving teens. They can't blame mom for the 11 p.m. curfew; they can only blame the "man."

The law black-and-whites all kinds of possible trouble spots for kids: trespassing and vandalism, underage drinking, selling tobacco or alcohol to minors, possession of illegal substances, speeding. If you use it to your advantage, it's like having the Enforcer as your spouse.

The cell phone ban has been criticized for not being easy to enforce. I fear that misses the point for I always taught my son it's what you do when no one is looking that's the true measure of character.

GI JOE IS NAKED

Naked GI-Joe is in the house. Actually, he's in my sister's house. However, when he and several of his clones lived with us, they were always clothed. But since they have been residing with my sister's two sons, ages 5 and 6, they have been donning nothing but birthday suits, perhaps on imaginary leave to a nudie camp.

That's just one of the reasons my son has yet to forgive me for giving away his pristine collection of GI Joes, complete with jeep, camo-decored boat, change of military garb and an arsenal that would make a Minuteman envious. It's a sore topic as he recalls in great emotional detail the care he gave to his mini-platoon of Joes during their time with him.

He neglects to acknowledge they lived squished on top of each other in a large Tupperware container in the basement for almost 10 years, forgotten and forlorn with no one to play with them. While he moved on to video games, drum sets and electronic gadgetry, the Joes lay dormant and unloved. Now, naked or not, they are loved and played with, known as a favorite toy given to them by their revered older cousin. You can't buy that type of adoration.

Now before you get your knickers in a twist, I don't just give away my son's old toys willy-nilly. There are racks and racks of beautiful books, baby, toddler and otherwise, awaiting his progeny if he should have any. A hand-carved, push giraffe my grandfather gave him; his favorite stuffed crib toy; a canvas bag of wooden blocks, and prized possessions from his growing years. I even have a wooden dollhouse sans furniture that he used to play with and a toy chest full of odds and ends that he chooses to hang onto rather than sort through. If he were to open it, I am certain he would find little worth saving, save those toys that evoke a sadness and sentimentality about how the years have flown by. I have had more than my share of reminders of that.

My belief is that toys should be played with and enjoyed. But my son is a saver, a packrat, an 'I-might-need-this-one-day' hoarder in the making. While he has in the past shown shrugged indifference to most of the toys I have asked him to hand over to his little cousins, all of a sudden, he now cares. Not one more toy must leave this house to go to anyone. Ever. Period.

It's "Toy Story 3" in reverse. Not that I have seen the movie, but friends and even some of my column readers have recommended I see it with my son as he prepares to run screaming from the prison that is his home to the free and easy life at college.

But I refuse to see this movie. And it's not because I don't want to cry. I love crying. But I doubt seeing the movie will be enough to change his mind.

I think knowing that GI Joe is naked is just more than he can bear.

TEEN SPEAK

It's a matter of linguistics when you come right down to it. Sometimes disagreements can boil down to simple miscommunication. I came to this conclusion when trying to determine why my teenage son and I have problems seeing eye-to-eye on very basic day-to-day happenings. I forced myself to dissect the way we communicate because it doesn't take much to put him on the defensive. While I used to chalk that up to pubescent touchiness, it dawned on me that perhaps I wasn't fully understanding him. He seemed to be speaking another language even though the words sounded quite familiar. It was a language that I needed to learn.

Over time, I have realized that the words and phrases he uses have different meanings than I am used to. For instance, his idea of "soon" is my idea of "later." Especially when used in response to questions such as, "When will you be finished with your homework?" He responds: "Soon," which would indicate to me that he will be done in a relatively short period of time. But this is not the case, in his culture, "soon" is roughly two hours.

That being the case, it didn't take much to surmise that "later" basically means "never." This often applies when I ask when he will complete any chore-like activity such as cleaning his room, putting away laundry and the like. "Later." Never going to happen.

Phrases as well as words also have other meanings—often times the opposite of what the ear perceives. "I've got it under control" actually means the contrary. It means he has given the task at hand a cursory reflection, but has no concrete plan whatsoever to accomplish it. When he says this, its actual meaning is, "Get off my back."

Two phrases that are interchangeable are "What are you talking about?" and "Are you serious?" Said with incredulity touched with disdain, these phrases are meant to get me to question my own sanity. These are what I call deflections, because he is completely avoiding the discussion by putting the onus back on me. In reality, when I hear these phrases I know I have hit pay dirt. Whatever the topic I am discussing is one that he wants to avoid therefore worth pursuing.

The most famous misunderstood phrase of all is the trickiest because all parents have the tendency to fall for it. "You don't trust me." Again, this is phrase doesn't not mean what we think it means. The tendency in response to this would be to defend ourselves and our actions assuming to smooth over concerns of lack of trust. The truth is trust is not the issue. The statement is really meant to evoke guilt; to get us to agree to whatever it is they are asking for. It's usually a last ditch effort to get their way.

Rather than falling into this trap, I fight fire with fire. "Oh, I trust you alright. The problem is: you don't trust me."

LET'S TALK ABOUT POT

Let's talk about pot. My impression is that there's been a lot of chit chat in the media and elsewhere about the innocence of this illegal drug. Except for the "Reefer Madness" generation, weed has enjoyed a benign reputation for a long time thanks in part to the carryover of the feel-good, hippie era, of which I experienced only the tail end. The discussion is more vocal now. It has been prompted in part by our new president and his reported views on limited legalization of this drug for medical use.

Let's put all of that aside. I am asking you to move it mentally off the table for a few minutes. Let's forget the drug is still illegal. Forget about the debate over its reputation as an entry level drug which has led many to using harder and more highly addictive drugs. Forget about the positive rhetoric from users and legalization proponents. Forget about the negative, fear-based rap it gets from opponents. Forget about the moral implications, if there are any. Forget about the unfairness of it all, especially when alcohol and cigarettes, arguably very addictive substances, are being sold on the open market and pot can land you in jail. Let's even forget about the privacy argument about what you do behind closed doors that doesn't hurt anyone. Forget all of this.

Let's talk about the whys. Why does anyone smoke dope, drink booze, play the slots regularly, shop compulsively, binge eat, watch seven hours of television at night, or even exercise every day? It's a way to cope; something to help siphon off the stress. But like habits, some stress-relievers are not so healthy. And some, mostly the unhealthy ones, give you instant gratification. No matter how you want to package it, some ways of coping with stress do more than just help you feel good; they exact a toll in terms of dependency and can often times develop into full-blown addictions.

Let's talk about parenting. Like many others, I have spent an inordinate amount of useless worry and countless hours preparing my son for the onslaught of teenage years. It feels almost like a battle at times; any help from outside sources is accepted and gratefully embraced. To that end, I don't need to hear about the innocence of any addictive behavior, whether it be nail biting, eating pork rinds or pot smoking. Especially when it affects someone like my son who is a member of a unique population that has yet to develop the maturity and experience to know any better.

Let's talk about tools to learn how to deal with stress and the inevitability of life's disappointments and hurts. Let's talk about how actually feeling pain will not kill you. Let's talk about how nothing that provides temporary relief is ever a permanent solution for dealing with reality.

CHOOSE ME

"Choose me! Choose me!" From back in the days of being picked for a painful game of Red Rover right now to the present, this phrase is one we all have cried, either internally or right out loud. Whether it be seeking a job, extending a hand to a potential sweetheart, or lining up for our spot in history, we have all wanted to be given the nod on more than one occasion during our lives. And we all have at one time or another been the chosen one.

As my son sends application after application to the colleges of his choice, I hear his internal plea attach itself to each and every one. "Choose me. Choose me." I imagine all of the applications flooding colleges everywhere over the next two months, crying out for attention as they lie on the admission counselors' desks. He wants so very much to be one of the chosen. For what, he has yet to know. This vague and exciting thing called college is as real to him as heaven is to me. To him, it's but a destination. Once he is there, he'll soon find it's really another leg of the journey.

All he knows right now is that hopefully one of the colleges he applied to from the 4,000 or so in this country is where he will be spending the next four years of his life. And along with his desperate almost manic desire to be one of the fortunate ones to be picked, is the accompanying nervousness that hangs heavy in the air over any discussion of the future. So much so that he hates talking about it. Confronted with any conversation about his college plans, mostly the fallback dialogue of some well-meaning adults, he has chosen the low road. "I have no plans after high school" has become his blunt reply.

While this is not what his mother would encourage him to say, it has become one way he can keep from focusing on that which convulses his stomach into twists and tap dances on his nerves. For waiting to be chosen is the worst feeling in the world. Especially at this point, when it is fully out of his control. Transcripts are sent, convincing essays have been written and rewritten, standardized tests are last year's headache and letters about his sterling character by beloved educators are signed and sealed. Now the unknown amalgam of chance and destiny will decide his future. That and the benevolence of the admissions gods. It's the stuff that defines suspense.

So we sit and wait and wonder if it all is enough as his application joins the others, jumping up and down, its paper arm waving, urgently shouting, "Choose me." And all the while, it's up to us nail-biting adults to prepare and believe our pep talk, as is the way of practiced parents, hoping for the best but preparing him for the worst. For in the end when the names of the chosen are announced, whether it be in celebration or despair, we're all in this together.

FUNKYTOWN

If life were like a movie, every major life change, each epiphany and climactic experience would have a theme song, or at the very least, compelling background music. The morning of my college commencement exactly 30 years ago, a fellow graduate stuck his stereo speakers in the windows of his dorm room, and blasted "Funkytown" across the campus. The music reeked of disco fever, the genre of the day, but the words, while hardly genius, seemed oddly apropos.

"Gotta move on" was the basic, mindless lyric. At the time, it summed up everything we were all feeling that day. That chapter of our lives was closing permanently and now we quite simply had to move on.

I have revisited that dated song recently. "Gotta move on" has become my ohm as I prepare for my son to move on and leave us staring at the empty nest that was his home. A lot of past tense has been creeping into my vocabulary.

A bit of wisdom imparted from another parent last year when I was panicking at how I would be emotionally prepared for this, has proven true as we close the high school chapter of his life and open a new one hundreds of miles away. "When it's time for him to go, he'll be ready and so will you."

At the time, I just couldn't fathom what he was talking about. Now, I have been given the gift of amazing grace for I was blind but now I see. The simple truth is that nature has continued to take its course. He has outgrown this home. He has outgrown us. We are like diapers and booster seats, dinosaurs and fire trucks, footed pj's and adolescence, all of which preceded us and in their wake, left the message that eventually, we, too would be outgrown. And that's the way it should be.

As he grumbles around the house, seemingly at cross purposes with himself, his behavior mirrors his own conflicted sense of where he belongs. High school, though once cherished, no longer fits him. Those last weeks, nay months, of school were like too-tight pants— annoyingly uncomfortable and ready to be packed away along with homeroom, proms, changing classes and SATs.

I know the particular angst that dogs him. It comes from the knowledge and anticipation that change is just inches away, but before he can grasp it, he has to finish this chapter. And waiting can be the worst kind of torture.

It's created an odd dichotomy in this person, prompting an internal tug-of-war that has manifested as impatience coupled with a painful lack of motivation. His growing restlessness has been evidenced in exasperated comments edged with a finely sharpened razor, followed by a hurried apology. Confusion, fear and unbridled excitement at the thought of what is to come has to constantly be balanced by the humdrumness of the day-to-day.

My son graduates high school tonight. While I am not so certain he will land in Funkytown, I do know he's gotta move on. And so do we.

GIVE ME A COMMENCEMENT SPEECH

The kids filling the seats of the Warner Theatre donning mortarboards and flowing gowns were the stars of the show. The pomp and circumstance was for them. The floral arrangements and diplomas were for them. And the keynote speeches were for them. As we all gathered and beamed with pride, wishing them high ideals and all the good life has to offer, we knew inherently, they are the future. It only made sense that on this milestone of graduation, they should be the recipients of all the wisdom-filled speeches laid out before them.

But after sitting through my son's high school graduation, I have come to the conclusion that commencement addresses are largely wasted on the young. While these bright kids have their entire futures lying at their feet, how can they possibly grasp that? I suspect, like my son, many of them are looking about as far down the road as September when many of them will start college. The idea that their lives are being shaped by the decisions they are now making is just too immense to wrap their minds around. Most of them live solely in the moment, which is how it should be.

I have yet to meet a teenager who doesn't think he or she will live forever. I have yet to meet a teenager who doesn't know everything. That, along with invincibility and shortsightedness, comes hand in glove with being young. As I listened to the keynote speakers that night, I couldn't help but wonder if their words impacted those young, naive minds as much as they did mine.

It dawned on me during his graduation that it's not my son who needs a graduation speech; it's me and my generation. Let's face it. For some of us, the Golden Rule has lost its luster. We are the ones sitting in the audience who need to be reminded that life is a marathon, not a sprint. We are the ones who often lose site of the eventual successes guaranteed by hard work, turning the other cheek and taking the high road. We are the ones who doubt whether it will all work out in the end. For unlike our children, we are old enough to know we aren't going to live forever. We realize all too well we are vulnerable. We are obsessed with the long term and refer often to this vague thing called the future. We have to struggle to stay in the present.

Yes, we are the ones who need commencement speeches. They drape the tapestry of the bigger picture in front of us that sometimes gets lost by our own tunnel vision. They give perspective like our parents did, reminding us in adages and handy, bite-sized bits of wisdom that nothing is a bad as it seems.

While the young are the ones who will eventually inherit the earth, the truth is we oldsters own it now. And as its stewards, we're expected to troubleshoot its myriad problems. Given that hefty responsibility, where is our pep talk?

PACKING UP FOR COLLEGE

It was panic prompted by a long exchange with a female friend that finally propelled my son into action. None of my constant nagging, of course, did a thing. As usual, I abandoned that tactic and let inertia take its toll.

Reading about other first-time college students taking over rooms of their homes with packed belongings seems too strange to me. There is no sign of impending departure at my home.

Why? Well, in my son's mind, college is a destination: Utopia, marked by independence, free-floating fun times with a smattering of class work. No need to plan for that. Just show up. Details, shmee-tails.

With the self-assuredness that only an 18-year-old would dare, he has spent hours on what he calls the important stuff—social networking with other incoming Freshman, perusing the course catalog, deciding on what music to bring and whether or not his skis should accompany him.

With less than two weeks to launch, I have waited for it to dawn on him that he might need more than a pair of sheets for his dorm room when he moves to Nirvana. And sure enough, it has. His friend listed for him what was already packed in her virtual U-haul. She had started her list in the spring and revised it multiple times.

What my son doesn't know is that for months my husband has been quietly stockpiling stuff for college. Shampoos, soap, toothpaste—those silly things my son assumes will be provided in his dorm like it's a hotel—to general school supplies, room needs and other essentials. These things are mere footnotes of his must-have list.

Urgency lacing his voice, he calls me at work after arising at noon.

"We need to go shopping," he demands. I have never heard that phrase come out of his mouth before, unless referring to the music store or an electronics warehouse. He feverishly ticks off his list: a bookcase, microwave, refrigerator, drapes, shams and a rug. Clever me, I have already seen the online photo of his dorm room. I ask how he intends to fit a full set of kitchen appliances in a space currently the size of his closet. I am assured this will not be a problem. He is right; it will not be a problem as I don't intend to buy any of it.

"Oh, yeah, I need a shower caddy, too."

When I ask him if he knows what a shower caddy is, I hear his shrug over the phone. "No but I definitely need one." Yes, of course you do.

The next day, we are at Sears. Half way through the bedding aisle, I spot it: the elusive shower caddy. "Pink or silver?" I ask him. He balks in disgust. "Forget it. I'll just carry stuff in my hands." Reality takes hold.

The trip takes less than 40 minutes, yielding a total of three large bath towels and a 12-pack of face cloths. I can rest easy knowing he's ready for college.

END OF AN ERA

One by one, my comrades have gone before me. Mothers driving their children to college, either close by or hours away. Distance really means nothing when you are witnessing the closing of a powerful chapter in your life. Since my son's college starts later than the rest, I have watched fellow mothers for weeks take the lonely drive back from that final stop. I can't help but morbidly think: dead man walking.

Now, it's my turn.

Something I read 18 years ago has never left me. Parenting is the ultimate lesson in love; namely, learning how to let go. And I want to do it with grace. A simple fact faces all of us who have children. One day they will leave. Though there are countless times before that you wish they would, when it does arrive, you still feel unprepared. At least I am. And I'm scared. Not scared for him. Scared for me. Or more specifically, my reaction.

I know it's just wrong to be sad when he is so, so happy. And I am proud—thrilled, really—and filled with excitement for him. But as the time draws nearer, I wonder if this is enough. Am I kidding myself? I remind myself it's a process and at least I have made some strides. For instance, I have learned not to take personally his unbridled glee at moving out. And I never wax nostalgic over how fast time flies. But internally, while I applaud his independence and maturity, I simultaneously fight with my own heart, trying to hold it together, convincing it not to break.

The irony is that I can easily slip into his skin. When I left for college, I waved a hearty goodbye to my weepy mother, and never once looked back. Maybe that's what I am afraid of. What if he, too, doesn't look back?

I knew we were in trouble when he announced last summer that he was officially "done" with high school and wanted to move on. It's been a very long year since then. Though I know nothing about horses, I couldn't help but feel I had a wild one corralled in my house, restless and bucking to bust loose.

Advice rolls in like waves from the swelling ranks of my now-childless friends. I cling to all of it, still so unsure of what will happen when my husband and I drive away from his dorm—his new home—for the first time. I am hardly comforted when I hear, "It's not as bad as you think." That remark is oddly reminiscent of what I was told about child birth before the fact.

My girlfriend waited until she was in the safety of her car after she pulled away from the campus before she let lose the torrent of tears she had nobly held back. Hours later, she found herself lost in Dayton, Ohio. Thus I came up with our first goal: Finding our way safely back home, without him.

HOMECOMING

Rumpled, unwashed and under slept. That's the new version of my son that greeted us at Parent's Weekend. He was a sight to behold: Greasy hair covered by a woolen tasseled cap, two sets of bags under both eyes and draped in clothing that has clearly spent several months shoved in the bottom of a laundry bag which was never meant to replace a bureau.

Apparently, doing laundry, taking showers and even sleeping are not quite the necessary tasks on his planet as they are here on Earth. They are merely options that get pushed aside when faced with other, more desirable choices such as attending a concert, playing "fris" (as in "bee") and hanging out listening to music with his closest 37 friends. I just hope studying isn't added to his list of expendables. As is the way with college kids, he continually tries to bend time and has clearly convinced himself that he can.

But this new version of the 18-year old boy who left two months ago has changed—well, not in the most discernable of ways, given his appearance and still notable tug-of-war with distraction and focus. He has matured with a confidence and sense of self that comes only with being the master of his destiny. Or at least feeling like he is. He has taken to owning his life like a fish to water.

My motherly worries about whether he would become a boisterous party boy, a passive follower of stronger yet misguided others or an overwhelmed nebbish flunking out of all his courses have been allayed. One thing I have learned from my own experience and that of my parents and fellow friends with older children is that at some point in this parenting game, what we want for them and what they want for themselves does indeed intersect. The future becomes the present and with that, the affirmative nod that lessons taught at our hands do have validity.

It doesn't come with any pomp or thank you. It's reflected in how they make decisions as young adults, the choices and mistakes they make, and how they manifest their realities. I have always felt I was one of the lucky ones with this kid. Despite his stubborn propensity for trotting down the harder path, he has a conscience and a kind heart. And he calls home once a week.

The weekend was filled with meeting dudes and awesome friends who call far-flung parts of the globe, home. Kids who mirror some aspect of him, appreciate and share his eccentric and off-base humor and challenge him with their opinions and alternative philosophies.

As my dad would say, he is coming into his own. And as much as I have missed him and—now and again—have allowed myself the melancholic luxury of reminiscing about years past, I have to admit I marvel at the person he is becoming. It's just exhilarating.

Rumpled, unwashed and under slept. Yup, he's all that. But did I mention, happy? So very, very happy.

CHAPTER VII
TAMING OF THE SHREW

NO LOVE OF LAUNDRY

They say life has two certainties: death and taxes. I would like to add one more: laundry. As long as we continue to shrug off the concept of disposable clothing, laundry will indeed be a certainty. It is inevitable, and there is no way around it. In fact, laundry is actually in the scriptures. I think.

In the beginning, there was laundry. Mother surveyed it with distaste and tossed it to the washing machine, saying, "Let it be clean."

And it was so. Sparkling and sterile, she looked upon it, all folded and neat, and saw that it was good. Indeed it was very good.

Now the problem was that Mother married Man and beget Child, and there was a massive proliferation of laundry, which I am totally convinced will lead us to Armageddon. I hate doing laundry. It's never-ending and tedious. After you do a load of laundry, it's just a matter of days, sometimes even hours, before you have to do it all over again. The whole process is just not worth all the work. While it's nice to have clean clothing, at the end of the day, it just gets dirty again. It's like my son's argument about making his bed. "Why? I'm just going to mess it up tonight."

Seems to make perfect sense—that is if you are a teenager, bachelor or person who spends a lot of time in hotels. But to the average, neurotic domestic, making beds is just a part of everyday reality that we have learned to accept, along with laundry.

Enjoying the task of doing laundry is generational. I know my mother-in-law and my mother never minded it, probably because they were the first generation that didn't have to beat it against a rock in a stream. In fact, my mother's partly to blame for my laundry aversion. She never made me do my own wash. She did laundry for 11 people, continually. So I never learned how to do it properly, or to enjoy a passion for it. Fabric softener, separating out whites, even bleach were strangers to me. In college, I worked out deals with my roommates to do my wash in exchange for going to class for them.

They say that when you marry, two can live as cheaply as one. That may be true—but the amount of laundry increases exponentially. It quadruples. And when you have a kid, it increases 100-fold. Never wanting anyone to see my baby's dirty laundry, I—selfless mother—adjusted my own clothes wearing behavior. Jeans that heretofore had been worn only twice could now go months before being washed. In fact, they could walk to the laundry room and toss themselves in the washer. I did, however, draw the line on underwear.

Through this experience, I have discovered that true happiness is being able to see the bottom of the hamper.

I CAN'T KNIT

Embarrassment, that's what I feel when someone asks me if the sweater I am wearing is my own handiwork. I am forever embarrassed because it never is. It's the manufacturer's doing. And I feel like I have let the asker down because I can't claim it as my own. I shared this emotion with a colleague at the newspaper the other day right after she asked me if I had knitted the sweater I was wearing. She laughed and admitted that she often felt the same way, because even after taking a knitting class, she still doesn't knit.

There is something humiliating about being a woman who can't knit. Or sew. Or scrapbook. Or quilt. Or do crafts. Or do just about anything that many other women can. This sounds horridly sexist, I know, but I think it's a remnant of my youth—a throwback to my growing years. I was raised during the dying days of the old Home Economics class. My older sister was forced to take it at her all-girls high school and was required, among other things, to sew a complete outfit and cook an entire four-course meal. Seems the sixties was still grappling with the rhetoric that girls had to have domestic skills in order to land a man and blossom into a competent homemaker and solid wife. Bras were burning and all I heard was blah, blah, blah. I wasn't ever going to get married, so none of it applied to me anyway, I reasoned.

But my mother knew better. She was considered a gourmet cook and tried to train me at the stove. I was hopeless, so she suggested I work with my hands in some other way. She gave me to my grandmother—a master seamstress who made her own dress patterns and designed for the largest department store in Omaha. God bless the woman's soul. She was saint-patient. But once we were sitting behind the Singer peddle sewing machine, it was boredom worse than high mass in Latin. She had a vicious if not obsessive addiction to detail and was painstakingly methodical. It drove me to the edge. But on and on she would plod, quietly passing on all of her tricks of the trade, the simplest of which I still can't master to this day. "Follow the directions."

By nature, I don't follow directions which is probably why I can't sew well, can't knit without continually dropping stitches, can't glue doo-dads on scrapbook pages that look any good, and why I refused for years to be domesticated. Well, my plans to remain single failed twice, so it was with great reluctance and not the least bit of anger, I was finally broken.

But learning how to knit was not a part of the taming of this shrew, which is why I deeply admire anyone who can pick up two needles and a ball of yarn and create something to wear. It's magic and I plan to keep it that way.

IRON MY WORLD

I love to iron. It's one of those domestic chores that I gladly do. Some people like to do dishes, others like to organize drawers, some like to cook. I love to iron. Oddly, I am one of the few people I know who does.

I learned how to iron from my mother when I was nine. She would hand me a laundry basket full of white handkerchiefs of my father's. An inveterate nose blower, he never went anywhere—and still doesn't—without a handkerchief. I would smooth out the small squares of polyester/combed cotton, and found great pleasure in taking something that was once crumpled and messy and making it smooth and crisp. And I hadn't even discovered spray starch, yet. Perhaps it appealed to my inner need to create some orderliness in my life. I would iron the world if I could.

To me nothing is more irritating than seeing someone all spiffed up and some part of their ensemble is all wrinkly. And I don't mean their face. It's like getting a new haircut, and not bothering to wash your hair.

I have carried my ironing fetish with me everywhere. In college, the boys would line up on Friday nights cradling their shirts and pants, convinced in my theory: a firm pressing before going clubbing would reap a higher yield and better overall response. Most women, when they're sober anyway, prefer neat and clean to smelly and crumpled.

I personally always make sure that what I wear is pressed. When I travel, I pack my iron, watering bottle and handy travel pack of spray starch. I iron everything before it goes in the garment bag; I iron everything when it comes out of the garment bag. Then I take one more swipe over it before I put it on. You've heard of re-gifters? I'm a re-ironer.

But while I am an ironing fool, and I draw the line at fanaticism. A guy I used to date was always crisply and freshly ironed— right down to his underwear. That was a bit absurd. To make matters worse, it turns out, his mommy used to do it for him.

Perhaps the happiest day in my life was the one when I discovered the dry cleaners. Growing up, I thought that only my father's suits and my mothers spangly dresses warranted a trip to that exotic place, which always smelled like hot steam to me. As I grew older, I realized that my compadres, who felt ironing was beneath them, would send their stuff to the cleaners. It would come back flattened and hermetically sealed in plastic wrap, like frozen dinners.

I've often thought I was in the wrong line of work. Perhaps I should open up a dry cleaners. I already have the name: You Mess 'Em, I Press 'Em.

IF THE SHOE FITS

Have you ever done something a bunch of times that you know in your logical heart was stupid, but you keep doing it?

I have this really nifty pair of shoes. Dashing and stylish, easy on the eye—fell for them the first time I laid eyes on 'em. But when I slid my right foot into one, it was strangely snug. "Oh, well this is my bigger foot." Like most people, one side of my body is bigger than the other. (At least I think it's like most people.)

So when I purchased them, I knew they'd be trouble. From the first excited time I wore them, they've caused me nothing but pain. At first, the five-hour social event was just punctuated by numbness in my toes, followed by two warm spots on the backs of my heels. By the end of the evening, I was limping around with my feet on fire, refusing to stay encased in the dastardly things. Back in the closet with you!

Days passed. Once in a while, when rifling through my oh-so-many outfits, I would glance down. They looked up at me, innocent and pretty, tempting me. I finally gave in, my mind going into justification overdrive. "They probably just needed to be stretched out." "After all, it was awfully hot the last time I wore them, my feet probably were swollen." The monologue continues. "They've had plenty of time to sit and dwell on their behavior." "The magic shoe fairies visited overnight. They'll fit today. You just watch."

Upon sliding my feet into their genuine cowhide uppers, I cajole my feet, already tense with painful anticipation, "See it's not so bad." By the end of the day, I can't pry them off my feet. Back in the closet with you! It's back to wearing sneakers for a week. But sadly, somewhere in the back garden of my mind, like weeds, hope springs eternal.

It becomes a cycle: taunt, succumb, wear, ouch! Back in the closet with you. I am disgusted with myself. But as the days go by, the shoes call to me like Bali Hai. I fall again.

But this time, I don't even get a solid thirty minutes out of them, before my heels squeal in pain.

That's it! Out, out tight shoes. A fool no more, I pack them up in a bag with clothes to be donated, and place them at a nearby pickup bin. As I stare at my parcel, I hear a woman behind me. "Oh, what adorable shoes! You're going to give them away?" I look at her. I look at the shoes.

"No! You're right!" Back in the closet with you.

THE THONG'S THE THING

Sorry to say, but what lies ahead for women like me is a life cursed. I have lived all these decades ignorant that a seemingly simple decision like what underpants I plucked off the bargain racks at the Goodwill was predestining me to a life cursed with the dreaded fate of VPL or, visible panty line. For only those who like an airtight squeeze on their bottoms can elude such a fate: thong-wearers.

Hardly a slave to fashion, I've never quite kindled to the thong thing, which I view as a ripoff of a G-string, or something akin to non-underwear. I personally like my panties made with fabric, not just elastic bands. I enjoy their comfort and flexibility, and the basic fact that they cover things. I like them to be forgiving. And I just don't trust thongs to be forgiving.

But never let it be said I avoid change. I have two sisters with outspoken opinions that thongs are unbelievably comfortable, and I had their word that, NO, they do not give a permanent wedgie. So, I relinquished and picked one up on sale at—where else—Victoria's Secret. I eyed the minuscule thing and slowly torqued it over my bottom. It lasted several hours 'til I could bear it no more, and ripped it off my body. I barked at those two girls: not only was it uncomfortable, it downright hurt. They discreetly informed that I was wearing it backwards.

Climbing back into the proverbial saddle of the fashion horse to, yes, try, try again, I rectified the tiny garment and lasted almost an entire day. But I spent it as I have spent no other—acutely aware of my underwear. I continually had to resist the urge to readjust that annoying string that seemed to keep getting stuck. It was becoming increasingly clear to me that my next career would not be as a stripper.

I packed the tiny swatch of fabric deep within the recesses of my top drawer.

It's hard to believe the thong is already 20 years old. Why it seems like just yesterday that a thong used to be a cheap, rubber beach sandal. But according to the oracle of scantily-clad women—Fredericks of Hollywood—sales of the thong have staggeringly outpaced traditional panties somewhere in the arena of nine to one. More than 4.5 million thongs are sold a year, compared to less than 500,000 regular, boring underpants.

Well, as I have been coined as saying, to each her own. And if the thong's the thing, then tho be it. But I…I chose the road less traveled by—and that has made all the difference. Even if you can see my panty line.

G.Q.

Eminem wears a tight wool hat pulled down over his ears. He is hip hop stylish and gangsta rap sheik. The rap icon can still get away with urban trendy because he is perennially young. He wears designer jeans three sizes too big, cinched down on his hips with four inches of pricey Tommy Hilfiger combed cotton undershorts poking up over his belt. The rap icon can still get away with urban trendy because he is only 31. Heart-throb Ashton Kutcher leaves his long sleeve Armani shirt untucked and unbuttoned at the wrists, tails flapping loosely over his leather pants. While his fiancee may be 45, he's still a twenty-something and safely metrosexual.

I don't think there is such a thing as men's fashion. It exists solely on the pages of tony style magazines, the Red Carpet and in the lifestyles of the ultra rich and famous. My husband's fashion style is stuck somewhere between the two C's: conservative and comfortable. My brothers think that a pair of khakis, a button-down Oxford and blue blazer will get them safely through any formal affair. And my brother-in-law thumbs his nose at fashion convention altogether by insisting on wearing shorts year round. Every other male I know plays it safe. Just the mention of the word "pink" makes 'em weak in the knees.

Fashion is the fine line men walk or choose to ignore. While they care about how they look, they can't care too much for fear that once they tread slightly down the path of style, it will turn out to be an abyss of no return. If you let your wife buy you pants with pleated fronts, where will it end? Clogs could be next. They might end up looking like Liberace, Elton John or Snoop Dogg. Gaudy pimp is a look, afterall.

Because of that fear or just not caring, many men err on the side of bland. Anything that creeps too far beyond their clothing comfort zone threatens their masculinity and moves them one step closer to being considered a dandy, or what my brothers would call, "Mr. Fancy Pants."

If men's fashion does show itself in my world it is largely with one population: teenage boys and young men awakening to their primal survival-of-the-species instinct. The need to mate translates into intense preening. But age tends to shift one's priorities. The older men get, the less they care about the peacock dance. If you have ever gone to a men's gym, you know that most of them are working out not to impress women, but to impress other men. And 60-year old men aren't nearly as impressed by a man with a crisp trouser crease as they are if he could dead-lift 200 lbs. They admire sweat. Physical endurance, brute strength and natural ability go a lot further than Italian-made loafers and a natty suede sports coat.

So I ask you: men's fashion—oxymoron or curse?

INK ON

I was standing at the counter of my local coffee shop the other morning, pondering the rhetorical question of whatever happened to plain old coffee, when the chap behind the counter asked me what I would like to drink. I looked at him and went weak in the knees. He had what looked to me like an I-beam riveted through the lower portion of his nose.

I was so thrown off I blurted out the first thing I saw on the chalkboard: an extra large pumpkin-spiced Chai with roasted anise seeds. What the heck is Chai, anyway?

I left the shop, a little dazed, cradling my cup of scorching hot Chai. It was disturbing to think that I had become narrow-minded. I started up my car, and gingerly sipped the hot contents of my cup, which tasted to me like weak tea with sweet milky stuff in it. Hmm, so this is Chai. As I backed out, I thought about why this form of tribal scarring was upsetting to me. Hey, I try not to pass judgment on other's life's decisions. Who cares if folks are impaling themselves with iron in the name of individualism? It's their business.

But somehow, this 'live and let live' philosophy seems to have wound me up in the minority once again. By not caring what people do, I somehow have missed the trend completely. So while the rest of the world has been out stapling, scarring, piercing, tattooing, ripping, slicing, riveting and carving, I've been at home, watching "Law and Order" reruns, my pristine skin still intact.

I drew in a long sip of Chai, as I pulled into the dry cleaners. How do people drink this stuff?

Most people I talk to either have a tattoo or a piercing or at least have contemplated it. I haven't even entertained the idea. It is as foreign a concept to me as purchasing a rhinestone tube top. I used to think that body art was a generational thing, you know, meant for Gen Y'ers, or something. Until my brother-in-law got a tattoo on his ankle. He's my age. He liked it so much he went out and got another one on his other ankle. And he might even get more.

So where does that leave me? Sitting in my driveway, dry cleaning in a heap on the floor of the back seat, holding a half-drunken cup of cold Chai. Any way I look at it, I just can't see myself with a tattoo. Heck, I can't even get myself to drink Chai.

As I reach for the dry cleaning, the familiar pull of the Cesarean Section scar stretches across my abdomen. It dawns on me. Hey! I already have body art! My one-of-kind scar, courtesy of my ob-gyn, five or six unsightly moles on my ribcage, at least 18 prominent stretch marks on my hips, and a festive scar on my elbow, thanks to a childhood mauling from our family dog! They're nature's tattoos. Now if I could only acquire a taste for Chai.

POWERLESS OVER POCKETBOOKS

With school starting, you might feel a little forlorn that summer is officially over. But look at it this way: summer ending means that a new season will be upon us. And with that comes new reasons to shop. And I don't mean for back-to-school clothes, either.

Shopping is a fine fall activity; one that I highly recommend to help ease you through the transition that, yes, another summer has gone by and you're still wondering where it went. Don't fight it, embrace it! See the fall fashions. Unwind as you rummage through extravagant extras such as pashmina wraps. Grapple with the concept of shoes made with real leather uppers. Pity the wasted lives of those who tell us what to wear every season.

But mind you, just because you shop, doesn't mean you have to buy. Take this as a warning from one who knows. I'll let you in on a secret. I have been told by those who love me that I have a problem with handbags. Funny, I never thought of it as a problem. But I do admit that I am just tickled to the teeth that in the next few weeks, I am faced with the wonderful prospect of actually purchasing a new fall bag. I have been shopping for it for months now, looking at a whole host of different purses, clutches, hobo bags, totes, pocketbooks and mini-backpacks.

My need to buy handbags started gradually. Like so many women, I used to own one all-purpose pocketbook. And I used it 'til if fell apart. Then I started branching out to seasonal bags, then bags to match outfits and shoes, and finally bags for special occasions. The way I looked at it, a handbag is a vital accessory. It literally becomes a part of the body, a veritable extension of self, the holder and protector of that which defines a woman in this society. I for one would like to honor that by taking the purchase seriously. I am not about to carry some old sorry thing around that likens me to Eliza Doolittle or, worse yet, Queen Elizabeth.

So the other day as I was shuffling through odds-and-ends in the back of my closet, I found last year's fall handbag—a sassy number in red patent leather. It was a larger bag, a tote style good for last year.

The niggling thought that I have a problem was put to rest, knowing that this bag served me for a good four months. I tossed it on the bed and something fell out of its red, gaping mouth. In horror, I counted seven smaller handbags that I had stuffed inside, unused, pricetags still in tact. Like an alcoholic confronted with empty bottles, I stared down at my truth. Step one: Admit that I am powerless over pocketbooks.

I think red is in this fall, don't you?

OF ZITI NECKLACES AND FEDORAS

A woman I once worked with wore a festive ziti necklace. It was loop of dyed pasta, about 16" in length, and crudely knotted on a piece of white string. "It's a gift from my son. I wear it because he made it for me." Part of me understood this. After all, I have my own array of kid's art projects: painted stone paperweights, clay pins and a signed collection of refrigerator art. The odd thing was that her kid was already in college. It seemed a little weird to keep wearing the ziti necklace.

But I had to admire her courage. Afterall, it takes courage to make a fashion statement, even if it is donning a string of multi-colored macaroni around your neck. It basically says, 'I don't care how silly I look, I like this, and I am going to wear it." That's a level of courage I don't currently possess.

If I did have courage, I would make my fashion statement by wearing a hat. The problem is that I have, what can only be described as, hat phobia. I love hats, but I am afraid to wear them. Heck, I don't even own a winter hat, which of all things hat-related, I could get away with because of its functionality. I am just too paranoid to put something on my head and walk around for all the world to see.

Perhaps it is because when I see other women wearing hats my first reaction is, "Oh, look at her in that hat! Who does she think she is?" It is clearly a jealousy issue. Wearing a hat is like wearing sequins. It sets you apart from the crowd and draws attention to you. And maybe I am not ready for that. How many times have I heard my friends and others say, "Of course you know who Bifty is. She's the one with the hat." You can infer from this remark condescension, a bit of sarcasm and the underlying theme—she thinks she's so special! Hats seem to define people and not always in a good way.

The dilemma I face is that I know I look good in hats. My mother told me so. "You have a head for hats." I now wonder if that was actually an insult. Maybe it's like having a face for radio. Maybe what she really meant is that my head is strange-shaped and it would be less conspicuous if I camouflaged it in a hat. My mother came from an era when hats were in vogue. So were girdles for that matter. There are numerous black and whites of her wearing her spring hat to church at Easter time or donning a sassy little pill box when going out for an evening on the town.

Like my former coworker, I would wear anything my son gave me. Maybe he will give me a hat. Then I would have to wear it out. As long as it isn't made out of ziti.

THEY LAUGH ALIKE, THEY TALK ALIKE

There was a fashion trend about thirty years ago that swept through the country. Mothers were overtaken with the strong desire to dress their same sex children in the duplicate outfits. After having one daughter and a son, my mother fell slave to this when I was born.

I am not quite sure where this comes from, this need to have sameness amongst your children. Since I only have one child, I have never been faced with the dilemma of dressing more than one child at a time.

Being dressed exactly like your sister is bad enough. But my mother took it one step further. She was handy with a sewing machine, so there was no end to the possibilities when it came to creating matching wardrobes. While you're at it, whip one up for Mom, too. There is one photo in which not only my sister and I are wearing the same plaid jumper, so is Mom. We even had the same haircuts. The family Stepford. The only thing marring the mirror image was me. I insisted on wearing a white belt across my jumper, creating a waistline where none existed. Clearly a feeble attempt at individuality. Things got a little carried away when my grandmother made a matching plaid jumper for my doll. The line had to be drawn somewhere.

When you wear the same outfit as your sister in public, it draws the obvious question from onlookers: Are they twins? This comment underscores the widely held belief that no one in her right mind would dress kids exactly alike unless they were indeed twins. Isn't that the farthest thing from the truth? My older sister has five years on me. Her height alone was a strong indicator that we were not twins, and if we were, I was severely stunted.

It's not that I minded the clothes. The jumpers were spiffy and matching knee socks probably bothered my older sister a lot more than me. It was the idea of intentionally wearing the same thing as someone else that just felt weird. My mother must have thought it was cute, or endearing, or even darling. Or maybe she just wanted to have twins herself. But I didn't like it, and my older sister must have hated it. Nothing like having a little sister cloned in your own image and likeness.

By the time my mother had my two younger brothers, who were born blissfully less than 2 years apart, she shifted her twin fixation onto them. It worked better with the boys because they were fashion oblivious. They didn't care if you draped old sack cloths over them. I don't think they ever looked down.

I went from being dressed like a twin to wearing a uniform for 12 years. It's a wonder I can even dress myself in the morning.

NO GARMENT LEFT BEHIND

My underwear is strewn across the JW Marriott Hotel in Washington, DC.

Let me start at the beginning. It was the usual type of trip for us—five days of what would be a combination leisure and business with social events thrown in. As the week crept closer, I loathed the ever-pressing need to pack for three people. I hate packing—possibly because of the looming possibility that something will be forgotten.

So I waited, as usual, until the night before, throwing clothes for every season and occasion into garment bags and suitcases, including half of my shoes because I couldn't decide, and then a few more pair the next day right before we left—just in case. Of course, I counted out my undergarments. But instead of packing them in the normal place in the garment bag, I came up with the bright idea to put them in a separate compartment, so I would easily find them. This was an extra precaution because I usually end up forgetting something—and it's usually something very essential, like underwear. Seems I have a mental block. I always take great pains to make sure that underwear, as well as cell phone chargers, directions, jewelry and toiletries don't get left behind.

When we arrived at our destination at the nation's capitol, I didn't unpack as usual, because I knew we would be switching rooms the next day. Never fully trusting myself, I rifled through the contents of our luggage, just to make sure I didn't leave anything behind. I panicked. I couldn't find my underwear. Not again. I knew I packed them—I just forgot where. After a massive fright attack, I finally found them neatly stuffed in the zipped compartment of the garment bag where I so conscientiously placed them. To my surprise and relief, my plan had worked.

The next day, we moved from the 11th floor down to the 1st floor. Upon unpacking, I once again could not find my underwear. Don't panic, I reminded myself of my foolproof packing plan. I whipped open the garment bag. To my shock, the small zippered compartment was empty! No underwear. Did someone steal my underwear?

It would appear that I had forgotten to zip the compartment closed the day before. Mortified, the icy reality sank in that all of my underwear was now somewhere between the first and 11th floors. And most likely, dozens of people had already viewed them. That thought alone made me nauseous.

Underwear is a funny thing. People are pretty sensitive about it. No one, except kids under six and Brittany Spears, wants to be seen in their underwear. It's personal. And losing underwear isn't like losing anything else, either. If it were, I could report it to Lost and

Found, or ask the bell hop for some help.

Sadly, a red-faced, reluctant reconnaissance mission only uncovered two pair of my underwear. What happens to undergarments that lay scattered through the hallways of a nice hotel? It's an answer I will never know. So much for my new policy of no garment left behind.

WHAT'S IN YOUR WALLET?

My wallet has become the junk drawer of my pocketbook. Out of curiosity, I sorted through this enigmatic black leather thing the other day, and I found I barely knew it. Other than an overused ATM card and my driver's license, it seems I never really visit my wallet that often.

Stuffed in its little side slots, I found not one, but three coffee cards (all for the same convenience mart with several punches out of each), two library cards (one for my son), a Blockbuster card from a store branch in Maine where my mother-in-law used to live, an old photo press ID from my days as a reporter, a AAA membership card—expiration date: 1997, two AT&T calling cards from a phone number three moves ago, and a discount card from an outlet store in New Jersey. One would deduce from this that I had a penchant for saving money.

The photo section revealed with horror that the most recent photo of my son that I have for bragging rights is his third grade school photo, before braces. There is another of my brother's son as a newborn (he just turned ten); a photo of me cheesecaking with each of my sisters (we all had our original hair color); several photos of my girlfriend's children as infants (all of whom are now shaving); a photo of a kid that for the life of me I can't place; my social security card (oh, that's where it is); and of course, more discount coffee cards. Boy, I must be desperate to save 79 cents. Lots of kids in my wallet. And they are all permanent, even the mystery kid. All of them are stuck like glue to their plastic sleeves thanks to time and the climate.

In the place where a normal person would put paper currency, I have receipts (grocer's, restaurants, ATM machine, gas station, even the convenience mart for my coffee purchases). I have become a collector of receipts. There is also a copy of my son's birth certificate, just in case I am stopped and questioned about possible abduction.

Oddly, there isn't one thin dime in my wallet. It wouldn't fit. The wallet would never close. Too many really important documents in there. You may wonder why I don't keep credit cards or money in my wallet. That would be too obvious. They are kept in two separate places in my handbag. My ingenious plan to foil thieves. Any pickpocket sorry enough to steal my wallet would find no money, no plastic, just an assortment of old gummy-faced baby photos.

This was a fact-finding expedition, not a clean sweep, so I put everything carefully back in its place. Who knows, some day I might just need all of it. And if I did empty my wallet, what would I have to put in it? All my stuff would be gone.

CHAPTER VIII
DEAR DAD
AS SERIES OF REMEMBRANCES AND LETTERS TO MY DECEASED FATHER

My father was born in 1926 in Omaha, Nebraska. He always had kindredship with Johnny Carson, another fine Nebraska boy who done good. When my dad moved to New York City at barely 21, he was still pulling hay out of his hair. He spent his entire life joking about being a hick from Omaha. It was also his favorite putdown when someone was acting dim-witted, especially his children. "Okay, Omaha, let's try this again."

When he was diagnosed with a rare form of leukemia in the fall of 2004, the doctors told him that he was in the most favorable of positions, giving him at least two years. My father sank into depression. And I began searching for my miracle.

At first, I had a general idea about how this miracle should look. Cure my father. Simple, straightforward. Plebian. This was the same miracle I had looked for 14 years before when my mother was diagnosed with cancer. I knew better.

Then I tried packaging my miracle in a more specific ways, dressing it up in positive attitudes, stretching it with pep talks, arguing with it to the point of abject frustration. The miracle never came. Then the phone rang at 2:00 in the morning. "Dad is in hospital." It had nothing to do with leukemia, it had nothing to do with depression, it had nothing to do with anything that had come to be synonymous with my father. It was a mystery.

I decided that if I couldn't find a miracle, I would give him one of my own. At his bedside, I swallowed my tears. "You've fought the good fight, Dad. It's okay to go home now." And I didn't mean Omaha. He joined my mother the next day surrounded by his seven children. It was three months since his diagnosis. And a week after his pal Johnny Carson died.

At the wake, in between bouts of enormous sadness, anger and shock were my companions. I went from handshake to hug, listening to patent comfort that didn't make a dent in my sorrow. Until an elderly friend of the family, our second mother, came up to me. My anger about my father being shortchanged spilled out like marbles across the floor. She held my hands. "Your father and I spoke at Thanksgiving and he told me he couldn't do it. He watched your mother die and he knew what was ahead. Believe me when I tell you this, it was a miracle for him to go so quickly. It is what he wanted."

Just call me Omaha.

THE DIAGNOSIS

Dad and I got off the elevator on the 8th floor of the MD Anderson main building…anyway, we turned right off the elevator and in front of us was the leukemia clinic. Packed with maybe 100 patients, all waiting for their appointments, transfusions, blood work, what have you. It was a sea of sick, dying people. Some with no hair, all of them yellow, pale and skinny, some wearing those face masks that doctors wear, some wearing rubber gloves and some of them with large sarcomas on their exposed skin.

I got weak in the knees. I felt like I couldn't take a step into that world again. It all came back. The days of my mother's illness. That world, that place which is like a universe within a universe, another dimension where people are mutant, reduced to partial human beings. A place where conversations about diseases, blood counts, what new miracle drug is in the pipeline is all they have. I had forgotten that world. I wish I never ever had to go back.

What has become abundantly clear to me is that Dad has not yet fully accepted his prognosis. It's as if when we went to Houston, he was hoping that the doctors would tell him that he was fine, and it was all a big mistake. Unfortunately, the opposite is the truth.

He sat there, basically shell-shocked, fixated on what the only few words that the doctor said that he could grab hold of, make sense of. "Your chances of living more than two years are higher than most." Of course what he heard was the number—his life being reduced to a number.

Having your life have an endpoint is not what most people want or expect in life. Oh, it's easy to say that we all don't know how much time we have, that any one of us can be hit by a bus at any point. Phrases like that make an empty clanging sound when they fall on the ears of those who are dying. Even though my mother had an incurable disease known as multiple myeloma, we never knew how long she had. We never had the balls to ask the question.

Now the question was answered before it was even asked.

Leaving the world of denial behind will be the hardest part for Dad. Embracing and accepting reality has never been a strong suit. I asked him about this during our trip to Houston, and he said, "I am a winner. I never want to think of myself as anything but." He said that this was part of the motivation behind not asking my mother's doctor about her prognosis. "Short-term goals," he said. Focus on short-term goals.

I'm a big picture person myself. I don't focus well on the short term goals...I need to make it to the end. Two years...two years is a long time, but when it comes to a life expectancy, it ain't much. I have been fighting with my own feelings about this, not fully allowing myself to feel the futility of it, to define in terms of that which is familiar to me. Two years...my son will be 15 and going to the funeral of the man he calls his hero. That's probably the most difficult part of all of this. Having to navigate these waters for and with my son when I am not sure I have the ability to do it for myself.

Two more Christmases...what do you buy a person who will be dead in two years? When my mother celebrated Mother's Day, it was two days before she died. I remember thinking we'll be dividing this jewelry up before you know it. How do you make every minute count when someone is dying? What do you do to make sure that you burn every moment into your heart, your memory, your mind?

It's not enough time. It's just not enough. There has to be something, something to help this decline. Body weakening, not strong enough to battle fatigue right now…soon that will lapse into the inability to battle disease, to stave off weight loss, to do much more than just exist, keep the body alive, the heart pumping, the lungs breathing. I know where this is going. I have been here before.

Right under the surface, there is a flood gate. It's right there waiting to burst open with a gush of tears and sadness, waiting to pour out in an uncontrolled series of wave after wave of grief, anger and terrible sadness.

I have to find a place for this. I have not allowed myself the chance to open that gate, that incredible grief. I am not ready to say goodbye. I need more time.

Dear Dad:

I wonder if Santa ever gets tired. I mean, bone tired. The kind of tired that makes your soul ache. Does he ever want to drop off that overstuffed sack of toys, board up the sleigh, kennel Rudolph and just check out for one holiday? I wouldn't blame him if he did. For I am at that emotional place this year. I am weary. I wouldn't mind skipping Christmas altogether. (Please don't tell my son I said that.)

It's not that I am not ready. For once, I am early. All the gifts are purchased and wrapped in that gaudy, glitzy paper of the season. Bows are affixed, cards stamped, cookies baked and all eaten (by me) and even the dog is getting some holiday cheer this Noel. You can tell that I have pulled out all the stops when even Bear gets a gift. Days were filled with shopping, shopping, shopping in the last month or so. Not because I had much more to get than years gone by. No, it was because I was obsessed with finding the perfect gift this year.

The dilemma is that now, even with all that fever-pitched shopping and silly spending, I wasn't able to do it. I could not find the perfect gift. It seems that I can't give those I love what they really need this Christmas. That reality has left me feeling completely useless, overwhelmed and bone tired.

You see, there will be a new, yet not unfamiliar, uninvited guest at my holiday table this year. Cancer will be joining us, along with its insidious companions, Fear, Despair and Uncertainty. In fact, this unwelcome coterie will be joining several dear friends of mine as well, and there is nothing we can do about it. We're going to need a lot more than a rousing rendition of Jingle Bells to make our spirits bright this weekend.

What I need to give my friends and myself this year can't be found at the mall, or the outlets, not at the finest department stores or on Ebay. I know, I've tried. They say the best things in life are free—what they don't tell you is that they are nearly impossible to find. Very few boutiques have joy in stock, much less at affordable prices. How do you wrap up hope? Does healing come in one-size-fits-all? Where is the perfect card that will instantly lift the sorrow of a burdened, despairing soul? At the bottom of my stocking, will there be even the tiniest of Christmas miracles? It seems my gift closet is just fresh out of happy hearts.

You know there just might be something I can give you for Christmas this year afterall. I can give you a wish. My wish for you and me is peace. I wish for peace in your heart, your body, your family and home, and in your universe.

And maybe, just maybe, if you dig deep enough inside your sock, you will indeed find a stocking stuffer miracle.

Dear Dad:

Well, it's all over now but the heavy lifting, I thought to myself as we opened up the door to the place you called home. Literally. The large oak table, mahogany desk, eight foot armoire, the king sized bed. Sweat replaced tears as the men grunted and moved the enormous furniture down the stairs. Mag and I sifted through mounds of papers, boxes of family heirlooms, closets full of suits, file upon file of saved bits of a long, multi-faceted life.

You were more than just the sum total of these things. Yet these things are all that is left of you in this world. I can now understand the why behind leaving a room completely intact after the loss of a loved one. It holds the imprint of a life, the essence.

If everything could be left in place, maybe, just maybe I could preserve the feel of you a wee bit longer. Maybe if your leather chair was never moved, I would be able to vividly recall how you looked sitting in it scotch in one hand, newspaper in the other, eyes squinting in that almost comical look. Maybe you wouldn't start to drift into that vague place where mom, lost to us 15 years ago, now resides.

Rifling through your personal homestead felt like disturbing a tomb. It felt wrong, but very necessary. I knew with each piece of paper I stuffed into the garbage barrel, with every file I opened and read to determine its worth, I was desecrating a part of your life. Throwing away something I would never be able to get back. Now neatly stacked and packed, parceled to different destinations, your things have somehow lost their meaning.

We were all looking for something that day—a piece of you. To that end, we engaged in too much pack rat-ery. It seems letting go isn't nearly as easy as saying goodbye.

Parent-child relationships are neither simple nor straightforward, making the grieving exquisitely painful. For some of us, there is the added weight of carrying around a lifetime of don't cares. It seems the tears keep coming and there is no place to put them when you can't turn back the hands of time. Where do you put blame and anger when the favorite target has vanished? Sorry doesn't mean much after the funeral. If I know one thing, it's that regret doesn't give much comfort to a grieving heart.

I was lucky. I walked the path with you, duked it out and made my peace a long ago. For me, you are a man I dearly love and will miss something terrible. The one person who was always interested in everything I did. You were my biggest fan. You were my friend. You were my father.

Yes, now it is all over. Everything, that is, except the heavy lifting.

Dear Dad:

The canonization process has not only begun, it's on the fast track. Not Pope John Paul's. Yours. I knew it wouldn't take long. I've been down this road before with Mom. When she died of cancer, something amazing happened to the siblings, especially the boys. Their not-so-blessed memories of her were slowly and summarily wiped out—replaced by ethereal images of mother of the year. I chuckle to myself when I listen to the airbrushed stories of this one-dimensional version of my mother, who, with all that fire in her belly, was so much more.

The Holy See waits five years after you're dead before the canonization process can officially begin, and then it is a tedious one involving investigations and even an examination by nine theologians who give their vote. If the majority are in favor, the cause is passed on for examination by cardinals and bishops who are members of the congregation. Unlike the Holy See, our family skips all that. But we do uphold some of the other protocol, such as the proof of miracles in the saint-elect's life.

Dad, you were full of miracles. You could steer the old Bonneville with just your knees, buy mom a lavish piece of jewelry the day you quit your job, and bounce this kid on your lap while singing dirty army ditties that even cracked a smile out of Grandma.

You could also scoop us up with one arm, drop us over a propped knee like a sack of soggy potatoes, and administer a stinging spanking before we could cry "uncle." Your "my way or no way" philosophy of child-rearing was unbending and intolerant. Thankfully, you mellowed as you aged.

This was perhaps the biggest miracle of all. Some men just grow old. Others grow cranky. Grandpa, may he finally be resting in peace, just got grumpier with each birthday, pushing him further into obsolescence. But Dad, you became more integral to our family as you aged. Your advice and company were in constant demand, proving to me that in very, very rare instances, people can change.

Dad, you will soon be a saint. All heads will bow when your name is uttered. But I loved all of you, the good and the not-so-good. I love the many relationships I have had with you—the gregarious, tough dad of my childhood; the devil's advocate of my coming of age; the touchstone of my young adulthood and favorite friend in my middle age.

You know, it's funny. When someone dies, you think about them a lot more than when they are alive. So, in a sense, they are actually with you all the time. Given that, I look forward to this new relationship with you as my constant companion for the rest of my life.

꧁

Dear Dad:

We are all back in the old house, or what some in our family call "the big house." To me that makes it sound like Alcatraz. It's moving day. There we are packing up rooms, sorting through junk and boxing the mess that was our collective life for three decades. It's strange that all seven of us are there together.

Seated in a comfortable armchair, is you. You ask me for a glass of ice water. I turn to the fridge to accommodate and it hits me. Wait a minute. You're dead. I rush to turn around and you are standing in front of me, tall and strong again, arms outstretched. I fall into your embrace and you hug me with all the energy of a young man. I feel like a little girl. I weep the uncontrollable tears of grief and sadness, knowing I will never see you again.

I wake up crying—those dry, gasping sobs that accompany fitful sleeps. I am lying in bed, but the pressure of your hug is so alive, so strong, it lingers for days. It takes my breath away.

The psychic tells me you are supremely happy. She says you never had a moment on this earth when you weren't worried about something. Now that you are in what she called the non-physical realm, you haven't a care in the world.

I would never describe you as a burdened soul. There are some people who carry the weight of the world on their shoulders, and made sure that everyone knows it. You had grace. You were always upbeat, optimistic, and had the world by a string. Even when mom was dying of cancer, you always gave her your generous smile to embrace her and assure her that everything was going to be fine. After she died, that smile and your fierce determination that the world was still a very good place to be, helped you live another fifteen years.

When you were dying last year, Bernie rushed to the hospital from his home in California to see you on your deathbed. He brought with him a handmade card from his eight-year-old daughter. We placed it near your casket. It was a good-bye card, even though he had not told her that her Grandpa was dying. It read that even though she would miss you very much, she was so happy for you because now you could be with Grandma Irene. Above the child scrawled note, she drew a yellow sun with light beams touching a small cloud. Standing on the cloud were two little stick figures, waving.

That's how I like to see my parents. And sometimes, when I look up to the sky, if I look hard enough, I can see you and Mom waving at me.

↵

Dear Dad:

How many more times will I walk by the buffet between the kitchen and dining room and knock over half of the sympathy cards sent to me after your death? The long, narrow surface is stacked with cards, many defying gravity, taunted by the floor below. The breeze in my hurried wake is the usual culprit for the flurry of Hallmarks that cascade to the ground silently like butterfly wings.

I must pick up the fallen comrades, veterans of the emotional battles that I have waged with grief. They are heavy with emotion and overwhelm me. My nose stuffs, and I've realized in the last two months that my nose leaks when I cry. I have learned to hold back the tears, but that leaky nose betrays me every time. Tissues are my constant companion to tame that traitor, for I don't like to cry. I am afraid to because the tears are always there, just under the surface. A surface that is so thin at times that any tiny crack will unleash the dam.

My son cries silently at night. Right before falling asleep. His nose belies him as well. I hear him sniffling. He has learned to sleep with a tissue box instead of a night light. When I cry with him, my tears flow not from sadness but frustration. Not having answers, I have nothing to comfort him with but tears and a runny nose. We blow our tissues, serenading each other into emotional exhaustion.

My son never looks at the cards for you. He walks silently past the paper memorial. The cards have been there so long, I, too, no longer really see them. But once removed, that space will be empty. And I will indeed notice that, for something will be missing. The emptiness will be a constant reminder of what I have lost. And right now, I just can't bear that.

It's been two months. Like Christmas lights that still grace a house long past Yuletide, these cards are past their season. What would Miss Manners say? Surely there must be a timeline for grieving. But when does the biting emptiness of loss give way to the milder, sorrowful ache? I used to know the answer. I have been here before, but can't seem to remember. I wonder why it is that we have to relearn how to grieve every time around.

So if the bulging press of sympathy cards allows me to dwell in the land of the in-between, somewhere between complete denial and full acceptance of the stark, sad, inevitable truth that you're really, really gone, then please indulge me. Let me keep my house of cards for as long as I can.

Dear Dad:

I had a visit from you the other day. Strange, since you've been dead since January. But true, since I've been talking to you daily and you had to surface sooner or later. Even if it was just to tell me to "pipe down."

If you ever had a loved one die, you can understand how the nature of that relationship changes, and it really doesn't end at all. It just transforms into something else, something much more subtle.

I didn't always believe this. When Mom passed away 15 years ago, I honestly thought she left me. My grief was so all-consuming. I had visited her every day that she was in the hospital to bring her coffee and a Boston creme donut. Cancer had changed her so much physically that her vanity wouldn't allow her to let anyone photograph her.

After she was gone, I longed to have just one photo from all those months she was in the hospital. I kicked myself over and over again for not violating her wishes.

I was so focused on what I didn't have that I completely missed what I did. If she visited at all, I am sure I wasn't aware.

But as life steadily rolled on and over me at times, my perspective changed. Personal loss including miscarriages, the death of friends, the ravages of divorce created another dimension to my life. I firmly knew I had no answers, so why not be open to possibility?

The day after your funeral, you gave me my first gift. During our preliminary sifting through of your things, we happened upon the files you kept on each one of us kids. Mine was full of faded blue report cards—all A's, of course—old essays, birthday cards I sent to you and mom—stuff like that. As I worked through the stack, I saw something wedged into one of the folds of the accordion folder. A Polaroid. It was a 31-year old me, sitting on the hospital bed in Mom's room, my arm around her shoulder. We are smiling at each other.

And those gifts just keep on coming. Like just the other day, when we were finishing dinner and my son, who always eats everything in front of him except the plate, announced he couldn't finish, I thought it odd. When he added, "I guess my eyes are bigger than my stomach," I almost dropped my margarita. You, Mr. Cliche Man, used to say that to us when we were kids. I hadn't heard it in probably 30 years.

"Why did you say that?" He looked at me and shrugged.

Perhaps you could argue it was mere coincidence. Even if it was, I don't care. For that moment, you were there, at the dinner table. Another kiss from heaven.

Dear Dad:

I saw the first fall leaf today on the driveway, as I was trying desperately not to trip over the stupid dog bowl. Perhaps that humidity that always marks August is finally on its way out. That first multi-colored leaf now signals the end of what you always joke was a two-week season here—summer.

I thought of you today, Dad, as I do so very many days. Even though I have said goodbye far too soon to so many of those I love, saying goodbye to you has been the hardest. Maybe because you're my last parent to die. Maybe it's because I had the longest relationship with you. I don't know. I just miss you so much.

The funny thing is now that you're gone, all those wonderful insights you had into life are starting to make sense. Is it too late to tell you that? Sometimes I think I am going a bit nutty in the head, as mom would say. I talk right out loud to you, as if you are standing there next to me in the living room, cup of coffee in hand, looking out on the lake. Right out loud. As if you can hear me. Can you hear me, Dad?

I sure could use your help with your grandson right now. School's starting up soon, and we are already going through the anxieties of the damned. I want to bungee cord him to the bed until he cries "uncle" and agrees to get that mop on his head trimmed to a decent length. I know, pick and choose your battles. But the hair…it really gets to me. I know you're right, he is a good kid. But it really looks terrible.

I also want you to know that I am trying, Dad. A happy family was the most important thing to you while you were here with us. I am working on keeping the family together, which is a lot harder now that you are gone. Seems our childhood feuds have grown up with us, and several of us suffer from the judge-jury-and-executioner syndrome. Seems your 'live and let live' philosophy still hasn't sunken in. Letting go of grudges gets very hard when you're middle-aged. But I am trying, and it isn't that easy when there is no one who appreciates it. Like you used to.

Well, Dad, I guess that's all for now. I am not quite sure where to send this letter. Maybe like the Native Americans, I'll just burn it outside and hope that the smoke reaches you. And along with it, all of my love.

P.S. I really would appreciate some help with the haircut.

⫷

Dear Dad:

Call me corny, call me sentimental, but I like to celebrate—
everything. Maybe it was the way I was reared, maybe it's something inbred in my character, but I take particular pride in marking
changes and events in my life and those I love. My theory is there is
nothing too small in life to celebrate.

And so it is with great aplomb that I will celebrate my son's graduation, which looms large today. And in the face of all those naysayers
who chide, "It's only 8th grade," I say, "There are no 'onlys' when
raising a child." Every stage, every tiny milestone, even if annoying,
is short-lived. And it all ends before you know it.

In the face of all those who disagree, I say 8th grade graduation
is perhaps the most important milestone of all. It doesn't just mark
the end of a period of formal schooling. It marks the end of him being a kid and becoming a man. The door is quietly and permanently
closing on something called boyhood, something I have profoundly
enjoyed and will dearly miss.

In many ways, that boy is already lost to me now, with so few traces
left behind. I find myself reminiscing far too much for a middle-aged
woman. Yes, the man-boy is changing. The cracking voice will soon
iron out into a lower register, no longer merely masking the child within but transforming him. Peers, cars, part-time jobs and girls will edge
out video games, family dinners, and movie night.

This is when mothering kicks into high gear, as it transforms from
the now-seemingly simple task of keeping them safe and parroting lessons of dos and don'ts, to one of finding boundaries, both mine and
his. For me, it is a delicate balancing act of restraint and acceptance.
Holding back my hand that longs to smooth misplaced hair, biting my
tongue that wants to nag, learning that a quick, half-hearted hug still
holds as much love.

The first minute I held this child in my arms fourteen years ago, I
knew the process of letting go had begun. It was only for a brief nine
months that we were actually one—our hearts beating in synch, his

tiny form nourished by mine. That was the only time that he was truly and completely dependent on me. The process of letting out the rope has been such a slow, sweet one, marked by small tears as he pulls away. The glances over his shoulder for reassurance came fewer and farther between, the good night cuddles diminished, and the kisses on the lips became unbearably awkward. It's all been leading up to this passage into manhood. And here we stand, perched on the edge of it.

So at tonight's graduation ceremony I will be sloppy tearful happy. You betcha. Even if it is only 8th grade.

You are the one person who will be missing; possibly the most important one. When your grandson plays his violin tonight, I know you will be beaming, prouder than any of us. I just know it. See you then.

❧

Dear Dad:

It's been remembered countless times before this weekend. In the fleeting feeling that a call needs to be placed to tell you some recent bit of family gossip; in the ache of not being able to get much needed guidance about a problem; in the sense that someone was missing at the holiday table; in the overwhelming wave of sorrow that comes so quickly and lingers too long.

The anniversary of your death is this weekend. Do you know that? 'Anniversary' seems like such a happy word. It feels uncomfortable to apply it to death. There is no way to commemorate such a day that isn't sad. And while it's officially been one year since you left us, our family remembers it every day. It has enhanced our personal tragedies. It lies there, not so much a fact as a feeling, sometimes dormant but always present. It's odd that 365 days later, the tears are still sit there, just under the fragile surface, a memory's breadth away from erupting. It should be easier, I reason.

But I have been here before. Several times. When Mom died four months after Grandma, we were blindsided. The pain seemed to never go away. We were young, then. Paul was in college. It was horrible and unfair.

I just assumed that when you died, it would be different. You were old. I was old. It would be more natural. I assumed we would somehow be prepared. I was stupid. I felt the same way I did when mother passed. It was horrible and unfair.

Nothing has changed but everything has since you died. We are orphans, now. There is no one in charge anymore. And perhaps that is the strangest, saddest thing of all. Whether we sink or swim as a family now, there is no fall guy.

My son has started talking to himself since you died. I heard him while at the computer the other night, an audible conversation with no one. I asked him what he said. "I'm just talking to Grampa."

Gee, I stopped talking to you months ago. In fact, except for a silent appeal for help now and then, I don't direct anything your way anymore. Most of my grieving energy is funneled into physically pushing down the feelings of loss that try to force their way into my throat. They grip my throat in a steely vice that makes it hard to breathe. But I will not cry. I will cry later. I promise.

Dear Dad:

"Every time it rains, it rains pennies from heaven. Don't you know each cloud contains pennies from heaven…Trade them for a package of sunshine and flowers. If you want the things you love, you must have showers. So when you hear it thunder, don't run under a tree. There'll be pennies from heaven for you and me."

Remember that song? Your last conversation with your grandson was about love and letting go. Though you couldn't speak your last few days here, you could listen. After you slowly kissed him on the hand and mouthed, "I love you," he asked you a favor. "Grampa, send me a sign, every now and then, to let me know you are still with me."

Mag has always believed in pennies from heaven, especially after mom died. Whenever she finds a penny in a strange place, she stops, thinks of mom and feels she has been contacted in some way, reminding her of her love and constant presence in her life. She collects these coins in a glass jar, as if they were specially transported from the other side and bear some ethereal power.

Mag was pregnant when you abruptly died. I don't remember what anyone else wore at the wake, but I have a vivid image of her in a sky blue maternity blouse and pencil black skirt, makeup washed off by so many tears. A sad truth hung over her. Our dad was gone... not just for us, but perhaps more importantly, for your young grandchildren, who adored you. And this little unborn soul would never even know you.

The odd thing is, from that day forward, the pennies stopped. But they started for your grandson. Now he is the recipient of these mystical, once-in-awhile gifts of a single coin found in the most unlikely of places and at the times when he needs it most.

Mag's new son was born last month. It was joy, love and fun all rolled into one—with an underlying, but never talked about, feeling of grief. Late one night, alone with her in her hospital room, chatting, she pointed to the empty chair in the corner of the room. "That's where Dad would have sat." Finally, we were able to say and feel what we couldn't earlier. For just a brief moment, you were with us. You were holding the baby, that enormous, full mouth grin on your face, saying over and over again what a fine young man this baby would become.

It was getting late. Time to leave. I grabbed my bag, kissed Mag and the baby goodbye, and went for the door. But before I left, I glanced at your chair. There it was—a shiny new 2005 penny from heaven.

Dear Dad:

For once 'later' has a date.

For the past few months, most of my grieving energy has been funneled into working like a maniac, and trying not to stop too long. It has been used to physically push down the feelings of loss that try to flood my senses with sadness and knot my throat. I suck in, force it away, and will not cry. Not now. Later. I will cry later.

'Later' has finally come. It's the 28th—the official, one-year anniversary of your death. It looms before me with dread. Try as I may, I can't think of a single way to commemorate it that doesn't require ripping open a deep wound that never healed.

It's not like we need the anniversary, anyway. It's been remembered countless times before this weekend. In the fleeting feeling that a call needs to be placed to tell you a recent bit of gossip; in the ache of the holidays; in the overwhelming wave of sorrow that comes so quickly and lingers too long.

It lies there, not so much a fact as a feeling, sometimes dormant but always present. It has enhanced our personal tragedies. And has tempered our joys. For on the flip side of every happy time, every bit of good news and tiny victory, there is enormous sadness of not having the most important person here to share it with—a larger-than-life man whose boundless enthusiasm for our achievements filled the room and swept us away. We're left with the sorrow that no one will ever replace that.

The anniversary of your death is this weekend.

I could ignore it. But you won't let me. And like wakes and funerals, as futile as they may appear on the surface, the importance of them is profound. So, too, is an anniversary. You can only push down the pain for so long.

Dear Dad:

"Count the Coca Cola signs." Do you remember us telling your grandson that each and every time we went to Archie's for dinner— all those nights when you would take us out because money was thin and I wasn't quite sure if there was enough pasta for all of us? "Count the Coca Cola signs." Those words sat on my lap the other day, just like my son used to. Not even four years old when we first moved there, he would easily bore when we went out to eat. Hungry and impatient, two qualities that only amplified over the years, he would whine right after we ordered. "Just count the Coca Cola signs," I challenged, buying myself, his father, and you, our favorite dinner companion, about 10 minutes of peace.

I had not driven by the old neighborhood grill since I packed up the house five years later. Strange. All the times I've gone back there to visit you, my car refused to drive through the old neighborhood, past the pub and my old house. Rather, it circumvented the entire area, adding minutes to the already long trip to get to your house. Now you are gone and memories just haven't been a good enough reason to go back.

Last week, I spent a few days near the tree-lined city where we bought our first home and set up house for the starving child and his new puppy, now affectionately known as Old Bear. It was not easy for me. But something inside me said it was time. I decided to poke the bruise.

The old house was a majesty—a large Dutch colonial with a tiny backyard and soaring ceilings. Inside the closet of the very last room on the second floor, that's where my son wrote his name and the dates he lived there. He wrote it in permanent marker. He wanted to be remembered. But I didn't want to remember. I drove by the house quickly with but a glance, afraid of the memories that would force me to pull over and cry. The house paint had changed, the front lawn was landscaped differently. It was no longer mine.

When my friend of 25 years suggested we go to the old haunt for dinner, a shy smile slid across his face. As I sat sipping beer, I found it hard to look at the barn board walls, still covered with vintage Coca Cola signs. Tears brimmed. I had forgotten this place, where you sat broad-smiled, listening to every word that came from your grandson's mouth, as if he were speaking in tongues. This place where my then-husband and I, still companions then, made efforts to overlook the troubles of the day. This place where the waitresses knew us so well, they sat down for a chat.

But there was no son, no father, no husband, and no familiar waitresses. There were just strangers around us, sipping apple martinis, of all things.

"You really can't go home again, can you, John?"

He smiled that same smile. "No, but you can visit."

P.S. There are 38 signs.

Dear Dad:

They don't break—a bit of your famous advice about raising children, and since you raised seven and a handful of neighborhood kids, you felt you were Dr. Spock and parent to the world. As I have grown into being a parent, I see that you are right. In fact, a lot of what I know about mothering, I learned from you, the master on one-liners.

The toughest part of this parenting thing is the nuance—such as knowing when to hold close and instinctively understanding when to let go. You understood this. You knew as we grew older that aloof didn't mean uncaring. It is a learned art for some of us parents. As you sat back and assumed the quiet shadow in the backgrounds of our lives, I now know you had to sit on your hands to keep from wrapping those long arms around us and hanging onto us for dear life.

When I was seven you taught me how to ride a two-wheeler. I trusted that as you hung onto the back of my bike seat and ran alongside, that you would be there forever. I pumped along Verplanck Avenue, with the carefree confidence of a girl who had the hands of a strong, loving guardian at her back. I peered over my shoulder, to see you far behind me, way down the street outside our house, smiling that broad smile and calling, "You did it!" I immediately wobbled the bike, and crashed into the oak tree that had jumped in front of me, slapping the pavement and skinning my chin. But I didn't break.

Mom never would have let go. She'd still be running alongside, holding my bike seat, if she were still alive. And I would never have learned to ride my bicycle. She was perhaps the greatest mother who ever lived in terms of fierce loyalty, booming cheerleadership and number one fandom. But she had some trouble with letting us grow up. One of her favorite books was *Peter Pan*, and I think she believed J.M. Barrie when he wrote, "All children, except one, grow up." She kept searching for mischievous Peter amongst our clan.

I am a lot like her. I once wished nothing would change—that my baby would stay small and gurgley, and I would be forever 32—sans 20 pounds. While my instincts are still to rush forward, check to see if the coast is clear, and then gather him up in my arms and carry him safely on, the trouble is, he doesn't want or need me to. He learned how to walk well over a decade ago. And he's just too big to carry. And while I have watched him misstep and fall, you know what? He always gets back up.

You were right, Dad, kids don't break. But we do—a million times over.

✿

Dear Dad:

How could I forget you? Two years ago, I would have said, "No. It is not possible." Yet, somehow a fear dogs me as of late that I betray my own certainty. And I am worried sick that I will—I will forget you. I already have started. Somehow, my memory has belied me, and my senses are failing me as I try to recall your face in the sunset on your patio, sharing a vodka and laughing about how life has once again proved us both wrong. The deep certainty in your hug—a wondrous thing that gathered itself about me and consumed my insecurities—is somehow fading in its warmth. There was a time I felt that it was only you who understood me, Dad. And you will never, ever know how much I miss you.

Somehow, some way, despite all my best and truest intentions, I have started to forget. Oh, please, help me stem the course of this tide. I never want to forget the intricacies and idiosyncracies that made up the you-ness of you. It is the least I can do to imprint you on the fabric of this lifetime. A lifetime that we shared, only in part, but oh so profoundly.

They say time is a thief. And, as usual, I find they are right. Will this thief steal away your face from me? He has stolen so much more already. I look at your grandson, this large hairy, lovely soul with a laugh so sonorous—so different than the boy you and I raised. I miss him, yet I excite over the future of his growth. You know he wrote in his 8th grade poetry book upon your death—the anniversary of which is a mere few days from now—"Words can't describe it. The empty space inside me where Grampa should be."

Are you still with him? I wonder is it you who is whispering in his ear, reminding him of who he is? I ponder if it is you whose hand I feel when the wind catches my hair and brushes the back of my neck. Are you moving the photographs of you and mom on my desk and leaving the errant penny in obvious locations?

For a time, I thought it must be wonderful to not have the strictures of your own humanness to border you. To be free of the pain of an ill body, reminding you of the boundaries of your life. But now I wonder differently. How hard is it not to be able to take the grasping hand of your youngest grandchild? What must it be like to know that the only memory of the amazingness that was you lies in the aging memories of your stupid children? I wouldn't trust us for one second.

I always assumed that you had the best side of good-bye. Now I am left wondering.

Dear Dad:

Your grandson has been a student of death since he was eight. Do you remember when his schoolmate's mother died abruptly? Unbeknownst to all, she had a congenital heart condition that placed her on borrowed time.

"Mommy, would you tell me if you were sick like Max's mom?" he asked.

"Yes."

He peered into my face as only an eight-year old can—a seeking, yet all-knowing soul.

"No you wouldn't because you wouldn't want me to worry." I gathered him in my arms and assured him I would live a very long time. He cried. I comforted him, but inside I knew it was not enough.

When you died, my son was 13. You were my boy's best friend. In the end, you were barely able to speak, your body shutting down slowly and systematically. Your last spoken words were directed at him. "I love you, son." And you kissed my son's hand.

It's been two and half years since the funeral. Late at night, I still hear him muffle sobs into his pillow. Sometimes I go in there and lace an arm over his shaking shoulders. I comfort him. But you know it is not enough.

When his friend was diagnosed with cancer two and a half years ago, my son got yet another lesson about the quizzical, harsh side of life. Over the months of highs and lows, he has been exposed to the roller coaster unique only to chronic, debilitating illness. It left him seeking that young, healthy teenage friend who should have been kicking a ball around a soccer field, twisting up enough courage to ask a girl out on a first date, and counting down the days to his driver's license test.

My son reaches out to him. He talks to him of serious issues—professional soccer, Michael Crichton's latest book, *South Park* and iPods. They play war video games. In this way of teenage boys, he comforts him. But he knows. It's not enough.

We embrace his mother; we cook for his family. And we comfort her. But we know, it is sorely not enough. And all the while, especially those of us with sons of our own, we wrestle with our emotions. For our sons are kicking balls across green fields, looking sheepishly at girls in Trig class and can't wait to feel the wind in their hair on the driver's side of the car. And we feel horrible. So we sneak an extra squeeze when they leave the house. But we know, it's not enough. We are powerless over what life may visit upon them. And upon us.

It's not enough to sympathize with this mother's pain. It's not enough to send over a tin tray of lasagna. It is not enough to be a sounding board. But it is all we have. And maybe, just maybe, if we put it all together, it will be enough. At least just to get by—at least, just for today.

❧

Dear Dad:

I know you've been hanging around as of late. I find the chair angled away from the dining room table, facing the lake in the morning over the last couple of weeks. All that's missing is your coffee cup and the paper.

Lately, I've been thinking. Some things in life are not meant to last very long. Summer vacations, rides on the carousel, Sunday dinners, walks with a best friend in the woods. If they never ended, we would end up sunburnt, dizzy, fat and, most likely, lost. I inherently know this, so even if I am blue when they have to end, I get it. But

I guess like everyone else, I naturally thought some things are supposed to last a lifetime. Careers and marriages, for two. And aren't our children supposed to grow up into adults so they can visit us in the nursing home?

You used to tell me, "Dig deep, Lenore." I'm not sure if that was farmer talk or philosophy, but I am trying to do so, now more than ever. When David died last week, I think the easy place for all of us to go was that purgatory of anguish—the underworld of the endless whys. I hate that place. It brings me no comfort and bitterly reminds me that I have so few of the answers that really matter in life. And the result is anger, sorrow and despair.

Loss, especially that created by the death of a young man, seems to create a void—a vast gaping emptiness that needs to be filled or it threatens to swallow us up whole. I admit I felt this when you died. But thanks to some deep digging, I took a chance on my hunch that you weren't really gone. Just a little hard to see.

When I was divorcing, which is a death as you once told me, and I was so worried about your grandson, you told me sternly not to deprive him of his life's experiences; that I had to have confidence in him to help him cultivate his own digging skills. I realize now—that's what you did for me. I often feel that in the darkness of that experience, I truly found my best and bravest self.

Maybe that is part of it. Maybe the void offers us the opportunity to find our divine selves. Maybe we are supposed to fill the void. We come in where the whys fall short, not allowing the lack of answers drag us down, or limit and diminish us to the world of anger and bitterness. Maybe we can fill the void with the natural state of grace that is burnished by hope and belief.

Until next time, I remain your daughter, digging deep on the other side.

Dear Dad:

"I found a box for Mommy." It was a relief, really. For months we worried over how we were going to transport Mom's remains from your current residence in Connecticut to her final burial ground in the U.S. Virgin Islands. Mom has spent her ashen days in an antique ginger jar. That jar sat in your bedroom, part of a small shrine to Mom's life and your time spent together in the physical world.

Even though you knew where Mom wanted to be laid to rest, you couldn't bear to part with the woman who had defined your life. While it took you all this time to catch up with her again, during that time you wouldn't let those ashes out of your sight.

Dad, I knew you were going to die a long time before you did. A matter-of-fact man with little use for anything you couldn't "noodle" through with your copious, expansive brain, you laughed away anything spiritual. When you cautiously told me, near the end of your life, that Mom was visiting you during your sleeping hours, I listened. And I choked back tears. I knew that your confession was more than just admitting you might have been a bit off-base philosophically most of your life. It told me that you wouldn't have to miss her much longer. You were diagnosed with leukemia several months later and died shortly thereafter, brought back to her arms at the same exact hour that she had died years earlier. Your ashes joined hers at Mag's house—stored in a slick, hardwood, masculine box right next to Mom's gentle vase. She always wanted to be buried at our home near the equator. And you wanted to be wherever she was.

Many a Christmas of my teenage years was spent far from snow in the sun. Many a memory lies in the sand of those beaches. When we decided to honor your wishes in a memorial ceremony at our beloved Caribbean homestead, the logistics of creating such a ceremony went from theory to reality. So it was a relief when Mag called the other day to ensure that the trip we will all embark on this week actually would include the ashes of both of you. Apparently, some law doesn't allow for remains to travel outside of the continental U.S. on someone's lap, no matter what the relation. I wonder what you think of traveling FedEx to the islands. I can hear you howling from here. When we board the boat next Friday and your grandson plays his violin as you both are finally joined together in the crystal blue Caribbean Sea, I will not choke back the tears. They will mix with the saltwater below me, and join you forever.

Dear Dad:

You couldn't swim. That thought dawned on Vickie as she was poised on the edge of the dive boat to release your ashes into the Caribbean Sea. Paul stood alongside her with Mom's urn. And for a moment, the irony of that fact struck a funny bone.

The late afternoon ceremony culminated a week of vacation spent with siblings, cousins and family friends at the island place you called your second home for over 30 years. Even after not being there for almost a decade, the sand crunched the same under my feet; the breeze, while hotter than I remembered, left the same saltwater film as it had when I was a teen. While tanning was no longer an option, sitting on the beach still brought the old question: When would the thrill give way to boredom? Funny, now I think boredom only exists in the summertimes of children and endless days of the elderly.

It was so nice that you set aside funds for our final trip to the Caribbean. Mom, the consummate entertainer, most likely channeled the idea to you. You wanted to remain in the place where our oft times tough-to-please mom was happiest. It took us over two years, Herculean planning and plenty of intra-family fighting to get you to that final resting place, with all of us together, save one sibling. It also took an enormous amount of love.

Before we launched out to sea on the boat, we gathered as a clan to offer up our own wishes and prayers to both of you. Friends and family, absent and present, wrote their wishes on small papers. Some were read; many were not. After the formal reading, they were individually burned in a conch shell. The ritual is Native American in design, meant to symbolize that the intent of the wishes would drift to the heavens on the wing of the smoke. The ashes were then to be released into the crystal blue waters along with you.

It was much harder than we all anticipated. Grieving is like that. Once you think you're all done with it, an errant moment grabs you in the throat and those age-old tears find their way to the surface once again. So it was last Friday.

Once out at sea, the wind cooperated as we reached the spot in the water within clear view of Mom's mountain. We all took our place, warm water washing over the lip of the boat on which they stood. The ashes came out easily, and were carried away by the waves. Your grandson stepped forward to release the eternal wishes. And as we stood in silence, small bits of the unburned messages created a widening trail out to open sea, following you to your resting place. The last charred word I saw drift away was "family." Your legacy to us.

_ℓℓ_

Dear Dad,

I am hanging up my spurs. It's taken five decades, but the time has arrived to give up. I finally figured out the concrete wall I've been banging my head against all these years hasn't moved at all. And my head hurts.

Large families, even though they are in vogue, are hard work. Not to say that small ones aren't. It's really a mathematical thing. Look at it this way: The more personalities, and in my case, oddball quirks, personal grudges and past perceptions of shared history that are thrown into the mix, the more complicated the dynamics. Exponentially there are more opportunities for squabbles.

My baby brother summed it up well this past week when he said to my son, "Your mother's biggest problem is that she's an eternal optimist when it comes to this family." While I hardly view that as my weightiest problem, he made a good point. Little does he know just how hard fought that optimism has been especially when there have been so many ripe opportunities and reasons to be negative, whiny and self righteous.

Dad, you were fond of saying that anger is a luxury few could afford. When I was a young hothead, I cynically dismissed you and your lousy, two bit armchair philosophy. But now? Now I understand the profundity and warning buried in that belief and I thank you for it.

Whether your other children believe it or not, I have tried like the dickens to apply that bit of wisdom when it comes to what Mom would have called "keeping the family together." No one asked me to. I did it on my own. But now? Now after many attempts of trying and failing, I realize it's an impossible task to accomplish. I can only take care of myself.

We have been orphans for over five years. When Mom died 20 years ago, it forced a restructuring of our family around you, Dad. Mom was not only the conduit of information and gossip to you; she was also the power broker.

It was understood that the shortest distance between wish and reality was Mom, especially when it involved your pocketbook and/or your blessing. She could also be the biggest obstruction. While you were hardly absentee as a dad, you did rely heavily on corporate managerial skills rather than innate parenting style when it came to raising this brood. You did the best you could.

When Mom died, all that changed. There was no replacement mom waiting in the wings that you could hire. You became the conduit not just between yourself and us, but between each of us as well. Over time, you never quite filled Mom's shoes, but you cobbled a fine pair of your own.

With you gone, all the conduits—save the ones we have individually created—have, too. There is no parent to lead, remind, guilt or encourage us to keep in touch. I guess I have finally learned that we have to each want that on our own.

Made in the USA
Charleston, SC
17 July 2011